UNEXPECTED
A POSTPARTUM MEMOIR

EMILY ADLER MOSQUEDA

DEMETER

Unexpected
A Postpartum Memoir
Emily Adler Mosqueda

Demeter Press
PO Box 197
Coe Hill, Ontario
Canada
K0L 1P0
Tel: 289-383-0134
Email: info@demeterpress.org
Website: www.demeterpress.org

Demeter Press logo based on the sculpture "Demeter" by Maria-Luise Bodirsky www.keramik-atelier.bodirsky.de

Printed and Bound in Canada

Cover image: "Breakdowns Can Be Breakthroughs" by Nina Montenegro
Cover design and typesetting: Michelle Pirovich
Proof reading: Jena Woodhouse

Library and Archives Canada Cataloguing in Publication
Title: Unexpected: a postpartum memoir / by Emily Adler Mosqueda.
Names: Adler Mosqueda, Emily, author.
Identifiers: Canadiana 20220495335 | ISBN 9781772584257 (softcover)
Subjects: LCSH: Adler Mosqueda, Emily. | LCSH: Motherhood–
Psychological aspects. | LCSH: Mothers–Mental health. | LCSH:
Postpartum psychiatric disorders. | LCSH: Mothers–Canada–Biography.
| LCGFT: Autobiographies.
Classification: LCC HQ759. A35 2023 | DDC 306.874/3092–dc23

Funded by the Government of Canada | Canada | The publisher gratefully acknowledges the support of the Government of Canada

This book is dedicated to my daughters,
Corazón and Juliet.

"Finding yourself" is not really how it works. You aren't a ten-dollar bill in last winter's coat pocket. You are also not lost. Your true self is right there, buried under cultural conditioning, other people's opinions, and inaccurate conclusions you drew as a kid that became your beliefs about who you are. "Finding yourself" is actually returning to yourself. An unlearning, an excavation, a remembering who you were before the world got its hands on you.
—Emily McDowell

Sometimes only fire can germinate a seed.
—Nina Montenegro

Joseph Campbell's wisdom: "The cave you fear to enter holds the treasure you seek." Own the fear, find the cave, and write a new ending for yourself, for the people you're meant to serve and support, and for your culture. Choose courage over comfort. Choose whole hearts over armor. And choose the great adventure of being brave and afraid. At the exact same time.
—Dr. Brené Brown

Contents

Chapter 1

A Mother Is Born

Looking to my left, the clock on the wall above my husband Luke's head read 7:15 a.m. Only fifteen minutes had passed since my last check. *Gosh, this is taking longer than I thought*, I thought as I did another abdominal crunch to the encouraging chorus of "push!" My OB, in mint green scrubs, sat down between my propped-up legs. Luke was by her side. It was at these fifteen-minute intervals that I checked the clock, again, and readjusted my numb lower half around my watermelon-sized abdomen trying to get more leverage.

At the next micro break in the action, the nursing team, led by my nurse, Doris, installed a large metal bar to the end of my bed that looked like the outline of a large headboard. Now, my OB sat within a makeshift picture frame. Next, a white hospital sheet was looped over the top bar, and both ends were brought together and handed to me like a rope. "Pull on this while you push," my OB instructed. Now, with each crunch and push, I also pulled, hoisted myself with all my upper body strength to the rhythm of the tension that burned in a circle between my legs.

The epidural I'd gotten at 4:30 a.m. had been effective to let me rest and sleep after the then twenty-four hours of labor. At that juncture, I said, "It's been twenty-four hours, and I still have to push this kid out! I need to rest or I'm going to wear myself out." The hypnosis training I'd done, religiously, the weeks and months prior had helped relax me. I still had energy but could not go on forever. The evening before, at 7:30 p.m., I had surprised the emergency department staff by calmly walking through automatic doors saying I was in labor. The initial triage nurse was kind, but I could tell she didn't believe me, saying with a condescending smile, "We'll have a check and see and likely send you home." However, as she pulled her hand out from between my legs, her eyes were wide as she announced, "You're 7.5 cm. I'll get you checked in!"

The hospital room was as nice as I remembered on the tour. The windows looked north towards green hills, which were a feature of the Willamette Valley in Oregon. Bright May light streamed in. I would deliver in that room and liked the idea of not moving to another one to recover. Luke and I had packed soothing chanting music to listen to along with affirmations—"I am safe, and my baby knows how and when to be born"—and others I played on repeat, as per the hypnosis protocol. The evening was enjoyable as I swayed and walked around the room. Our doula was helpful with encouragement and keeping me company. Luke had gotten food poisoning earlier that day and slept on the couch between major contractions. My labor nurse would readjust the baby monitor ACE-bandaged to my belly every hour or so. At one such adjustment, she turned to me saying with her accented South African English, "Are you ready?"

"Ready for what?" I asked perplexed.

"For the next contraction. It's a big one," she said.

"I don't feel anything," I told her.

"Now, right, now, do you feel it?" as she pointed to the jumping line on the monitor.

"Nope, nothing," I answered.

Next, she took my left hand and placed it on the taut side of my belly. "This, do you feel this?"

"Yes, I feel my belly is all hard," I said.

"That's a contraction!" she says.

"Oh, well, I don't feel anything other than that firmness on my skin under my hand." I answered.

She went on to tell me that in all her twenty-nine years of being a labor and delivery nurse, she'd never seen a mother so calm and not feeling almost two-thirds of her birthing contractions.

Some hours after these checks, I did feel pressure and lots of it in my hips and low back. At this, I summoned Luke from his feverish slumber to give me hard, counter pressure at my hips. He had used his knowledge of Chinese medicine while we were at home laboring with needles and moxibustion, the burning of dried mugward plant above various needled points. With the intensity of the sensations of heat and pressure, I gave short clear requests: "Harder. Stay there. Less now. Okay. Stop." He mustered the strength to give me the pressure I needed and listened well to my directions. This cycled on for a few more hours as I approached the twenty-four-hour mark.

The chorus of pushing support was nice, but it was getting on my nerves after forty-five minutes. As the time approached 8:00 a.m., there was a shift change. Now there were two new faces cheering me on, which I'd never met, alongside my OB and Doris, who had been with me all night. My annoyance with the chanting of "push!" was that it was not synchronized to the feelings between my legs. As a long-time people pleaser, I was forced to trust myself, my body, in that moment like never before. After crunching and pulling on the sheet for some time now, I asked my OB, "Can I change positions?" Almost laughing, she replied, "You're so close—sorry—it's not possible!" Taking a deep breath and putting aside the ends of the sheet I'd been gripping with white knuckles for over thirty minutes, I slipped my hands down between my legs, past my damp hair to find the edges of my vulva. The epidural numbed my thighs and legs significantly, but I was feeling the "ring of fire" as my daughter's head stretched an exit out of her forty-two-week-old home. Hands in place, I tuned out the dissonant chorus and tuned into the meter of my body and the pulses to push and rest that undulated through me now. Almost as an act of rebellion, I pushed when the staff took a breath and rested in the moments they sounded their cheers. In that space, I felt with my body that in birthing my daughter, I was also birthing myself. With each wave and urge to push, a chord within me, this new self would not always be in sync with the outside expectations and that would be okay.

A few pushes later, our daughter, Corazón, sprung out of my body like a jack-in-the-box. She landed into her dad's waiting gloved hands. Elation filled my body with a rush of heat and bubbles. With wet Corazón on my chest, Luke and I cheered, "Yeah!" as if our favorite team had won the World Cup. We did it! I did it! Pregnancy was over! I was relieved to be done waddling around and felt a surge of hunger I knew I could finally satiate with the reestablished space for my stomach. Love and joy and blissful thrill coursed through my body; my face was sore from smiling. Corazón's head of hair was dark, and true to her namesake, she had a heart-shaped birthmark square between her eyes. It was unbelievable—a natural name tag! She was perfect.

Moments after she cried for the first time, wet-eyed congratulations and hugs came from my parents. They'd spent the night in the hospital parking lot waiting in their car. My mother-in-law was on their heels and had not slept either. So many people were happy around me as the morning arched into mid-day and then early afternoon. I was still marveling at what my body, what I, had just done. After Corazón enjoyed warm skin-to-skin time on me, Luke took a turn, and then family and friends had their turns. The new shift of nurses helped me out of bed and into the shower. My placenta had birthed well, and my doula had it on ice with her to dehydrate and encapsulate for me. I would take my dried placenta as a nutritive postpartum supplement for the next few months.

Standing in the cream-colored bathroom shower stall, I smiled and laughed, still in awe or astonishment? As warm water fell over my shoulders and head, I held the wall with my right hand to steady myself. My body felt lighter and looser, and my internal organs began their descent back to their places of origin. Gingerly lifting my legs around the stall, I saw chunks of tissue fall splat around my feet from between my legs. Pieces that looked like liver lay crimson on the white linoleum shower floor. "Whoa!" I blurted aloud, causing a nurse to rush in.

"Everything okay?" she asked with genuine concern.

"Oh yeah," I told her with disbelief, "My body is amazing!"

That day, and the next, and the following week, I floated in wonderment and rode a high I'd never felt before.

Corazón was the first grandchild for both families, and the excitement of the day blurred my sense of myself. Shortly after drying off, my brother-in-law came to give his congratulations, and I was updated that my father-in-law, who'd been in New Mexico on business, was on a flight back home for the occasion. The air in the hospital room changed, and it felt more like a hotel room where we were hosting a party. A good friend of mine arrived and held baby Corazón while I settled into the wide bed, as if it were my throne. I was the first of my close, local friends to have a baby. With the birth achieved, I sat tall in my new status as mother. That room—with the north-facing windows, bench bed, and baby-warming station near the door—had been my cocoon. I'd entered a pregnant woman, confident in herself and her body's wisdom to birth a baby. As I swayed and swooned with the pressure in my hips all those hours of the night, the room had held me. Those walls witnessed my initial transformation into mother and welcomed me into motherhood.

With our daughter tucked into the seemingly oversized car seat, checked by a nurse, we gathered up our belongings and birthing props and stepped out into the hall to leave. At the threshold, I remember touching the doorframe and pausing. Here was the physical boundary, a portal, I passed through—first as a pregnant woman in my premother life and now as a whole new creature, a mother. My senses were heightened, like an animal, and my emotions were attuned to the environment.

At the car, I decided to sit in the backseat with Corazón. I urged Luke to drive home without getting on the freeway. My protective mothering senses were set to high. Heeding my request, he carefully backed out of our parking spot and navigated the parking lot, without incident, and turned left to drive home. Looking out my passenger window, people looked different to me. The world looked different. The sky was brighter, the trees were greener, and every living thing seemed to sparkle. Going along, we passed a park, and sitting up against a tree, I noticed an unhoused individual. Their clothes and hair were unkempt, and they had a bundle of belongings next to them in various plastic bags. My heart ached, and my eyes welled up with tears. What I saw, now as a mother, was someone's child. A child who'd had a hard life but had been someone's newborn baby. I looked over at Corazón in the pink fluffy baby suit my grandmother, her great-grandmother, had bought for her, and I'd selected as her going home outfit. The red heart-shaped birthmark that stamped itself perfectly between her eyes looked at me along with her eyes. The feelings that swelled in my chest looking at her had no names. That first afternoon home was a blur of new parent bliss. We'd left the house clean, which was a welcome-home gift from our future selves. We arrived feeling energized and competent parents.

I wanted to keep Corazón close to me and figured we could arrange things to safely cosleep. Most families in the world did, so it seemed the most natural. On our first night home, I felt armed with mama power and tucked a sleeping, swaddled Corazón in a clear space between our pillows. The energy inside me might as well have been sunlight. I was so awake, and I told Luke, "You get some rest. I'm going to stay up and wait for her to need me." To this he widened his eyes in bewilderment, rolled over, and quickly fell asleep. *I was made for this*, I thought to myself. *My Abuela had loads of kids and so did my Tías.* I had this.

That same week, I was up and around doing laundry and devouring the meals brought to us by Luke's acupuncture patients. I wore Corazón on my front, speaking to her in Spanish. It was my dream to have my child be bilingual from birth, unlike me. In those early days, I spoke to her in Spanish as she lay on the Pendleton blanket cover speckled with shade on our north-facing window seat. Her grey eyes would open wide as I spoke to her, and they would penetrate my soul. Then as an experiment, and as the speech-language pathologist that I was, I switched to speaking English and observed what happened. Next, I noticed her eye gaze relax, and she looked around, not at, me. It was as if she knew I wasn't speaking to her. She already knew that English was not her language. Spanish would be our heart language. We would take it back into our family line proudly.

The hormonal high and enthusiasm from the birth, and the newness of becoming a mother, lasted about ten days. As if stumbling down stairs, I landed on a new ground of reality, a little beat up. Nursing was going well enough, although I had real pain when she latched. In the middle of the tenth night, I barked aloud in pain, "Owe!" and glared at her as if she'd hurt me on purpose. I hated her in that instance. Luke saw my face of agitation. He had been trying to contribute to the mother-only task of breastfeeding but ended up just looking at us most of the time. That time, however, he swooped in, took Corazón's crying self away from me, and said, "You two need a break from each other" and then left the room. At he descended the stairs and turned further away, her cries muffled, and my panting frustration calmed. *Who was that mother? I can't act like that towards my baby*, I thought, before I flicked off my light and crashed into a deep sleep. Hours later, I woke to a warm, tense sensation spreading across my chest: engorgement. I slept that night more than I had in two weeks. My head felt like gooey pudding. Grabbing at my chest, I remembered I missed a feeding, and worry flooded my body. This woke me up and out of bed, and I went looking for Luke and the baby with urgency. Downstairs, I found him asleep on the window seat next to the baby swing. It was set on the lowest speed, and Corazón was asleep. Soft daylight crept in from the many windows in the room, and I touched his arm to wake him.

"Thank you," I said, "for letting me sleep. I feel horrible how I growled at our baby." After a pause, I said again, "I growled?!" laughing a little. Then my eyes welled up. Luke sat up and then stood to hug me.

"It's okay. Let's get some help with the nursing, maybe someone can come to the house," he suggested. I agreed but also felt a pang of failure. Disappointment twinged in my chest, too. My body had done such an amazing job growing Corazón. Why couldn't she feed her as easily?

A retired midwife, a mom of a friend, was invaluable to me. She came later that morning and helped me with the pain and the anger I'd started to feel towards my new baby. The white-hot feelings that flashed across my skin, when my raw nipple was noshed on the night before, startled me. Needing help was unexpected to me. The pain and my irritability were unexpected, too. I had birthed her well. Why was nursing hard? I felt silly needing help with nursing and for getting mad at a baby. I thought I'd know, or my body would know, how to care for her now that she was outside of me. Wasn't that how this worked? The midwife was kind and gave me needed advice about breastfeeding positions, cabbage leaves for engorgement, and how to repair the relationship with my new beloved. The midwife told me, "She's moved on already about what happened. You can, too. You can always start anew."

Not long after that helpful visit, Corazón was sleeping in a basket just feet from our bed. Before she was a month old, she was in her own room across the hall in her crib, still in the basket. Luke and I had tried different arrangements of cosleeping, but we weren't sleeping. Before kids, I slept eight to nine hours a night, and as more nights went by with less sleep, something had to give. My whole body couldn't relax if I could hear her moving around in her sleep. I loved her so much, and I needed some physical space to be able to keep doing the laborious thing called motherhood.

Luke went back to work that same time. He faded himself back into his workweek by working half of one week, then the whole next week. I had him teach me how to change her diapers because he'd been changing all of them for two weeks. For some blowouts that went down legs or up her back, he'd invented the baby spa. After taking off the dirty diaper, he rinsed her off in the sink with warm water. She loved it. With him at work, I spent the day nursing, doing laundry, tidying up, and watching Corazón sleep in her swing; occasionally, I took a nap. The weather was lovely that May. I went for walks, sometimes with my mother or both my parents, around the woodland trails near our house. As eager as they were to enjoy being grandparents, my parents gave Luke and me space to figure things out as a family on our own. How else were Luke and I going to learn how to juggle it all? I appreciated the space. I trusted my body and my female gender. As a deeply spiritual person, I mentally turned inward, and imagined connecting with all mothers present and past, for knowledge. I felt powerful when I did this and drew off of their energy, as if it were some sort of fuel that helped me keep up with the demands of an infant.

At a month postpartum, we also found a new house, as the current one was at the bottom of a blind curve. With a new baby, we didn't like the stress that flooded us when we tried backing out of the driveway. We'd seen the other house the weekend I was due, back in April. I thought it was more of a joke and a way to pass the time at forty-weeks pregnant than really house hunting. But what had been a whim of an offer turned out to be an answer to hopes of a different house, more sunlight, and a safe kid-friendly street. Two months postpartum, I was busy deep cleaning and staging our house to sell. Each evening when Luke came home, I'd proudly update him on my progress. Doing other home tasks than caregiving was a welcome change. The timing of Corazón's birth and the summer break schedule of my job allotted me a few months of being home with the baby. By July, though, I didn't want to talk about baby stuff anymore. I was getting eager to go back to work for a change of pace and scenery and to stimulate my intellect.

On a cool September morning, the kind that smells as if school is starting again and the warmth of summer has truly faded, I pulled up to a small yellow house on a corner street down by the fairgrounds. It was a familiar house, as I had conducted a year's worth of home visits there with the mother and one of her children as a pediatric speech-language pathologist. I had sat in awe of this goddess mother, three kids under five on the carpet and her glowing in it all. Lily managed them and their house—she did it all! She was a pro! On our last day of services, I asked her if she'd watch Corazón when I was back from maternity leave, and I no longer worked with them. Lily's tears of sadness that I would no longer work with their family changed to tears of joy.

Both she and her husband, and the two oldest girls, met me with smiling faces at the door. This was my first hand off of Corazón to a nonfamily member. The reality of that crept up my arms and left my shoulders tense. *That was unexpected*, I thought. After a kiss to her head of hair, I got back in the car and drove down two blocks to a training for work. I felt light and free not lugging the baby car seat into the building. I felt a little awkward too, like a sailor coming ashore after a voyage and swaying with the waves their body remembers, but which are no longer underfoot. Inside the conference space, I was met with warm smiles and big hugs. All but three colleagues were women and many of them mothers. They asked how Corazón was doing. Was she sleeping? How was nursing going? Wasn't motherhood the best? I nodded in agreement and sat down.

It was fascinating to listen to and learn new information. I liked having conversations about things and people that did not live in my house. My brain seemed to turn on after being dormant or hibernating like a frog in winter. Ideas jumped around my head and out of my mouth. I was back and in a familiar role as a clinician. It felt good to know what I was doing and to be doing something intellectual. Becoming a mother was different from being a pediatric speech-language pathology clinician, and I'd forgotten I was one until the tight burn of my breasts reminded me it was time to pump. I draped my chest and plugged the electric pump into the wall at the back of the conference room; the steady whooshing and sucking sound drummed on. As I sat with the plastic cups, shoved through holes I'd proudly cut in a DIY nursing bra, I felt like I was straddling two identities. I was happy to be at work, and I started missing my chiquilla Corazón with every cell in my body. After collecting four ounces of golden milk made by my phenomenal body, I packed up my gear. I decided that at lunch, I would go down the street and see her. I needed to.

To my surprise, as I approached the yellow house from the sidewalk, I was greeted with a crying Corazón. Walking over the threshold, I stepped fully into mama mode. I took her into my arms and sat down on the couch. In moments, I had her on my breast, as my own tears wetted her head. My body had known she needed me. Our connection was that strong. Sinking into the blue worn couch pillows, I relaxed. Being in the company of seasoned parents, I rested and didn't feel ashamed as tears still ran down my face. It turned out Corazón had refused to feed from the bottle that morning, and Lily had tried everything. Weeks earlier in August, we had started trying out the bottle to prepare for this day. She'd taken to it fine, but over the weekend, as if she sensed a change was coming, she'd started refusing it. I'd hoped and even prayed that she would take the bottle easily while I was at work. Not today. So after a good feed, I packed her up and took her with me back to the conference room. For the rest of the day, I stood and swayed with her tucked to my chest in the brown fabric carrier. "I can do this," I said to myself. I could pivot between being a clinician and a mother, no problem.

By November, and six months postpartum, we'd renovated our new house, painted every surface inside; all the while, Corazón was strapped to me. We finally sold our first house, and I was working part time. Since her birth back in May, I had risen to meet the demands of motherhood and well. Luke said I was a natural, and he was grateful I knew about child development from my graduate studies. Still exclusively breastfeeding, I came to own and assert that I was the best-suited caregiver. Our families followed suit. For example, my mother-in-law solicited my preferences about all things baby. She helped us a few hours a week and wanted to be sure she was caring for the baby how I wanted because mother knows best.

Taking on a traditional female role so strongly felt natural, and I felt capable. Over time, it allowed Luke to write a book and grow his acupuncture practice and complete his clinical doctorate as well as extended herbal trainings. I wasn't working full time outside the home, so it made sense to us. My mother did not model traditional female roles for me, quite the contrary. In my childhood home, my parents modeled an egalitarian balance. Mothering differently—traditionally—than what was modeled worked for my new family. I was proud to do it well. Life as Corazón's mom was amazing those early years. I savored getting to spend time with her in ways my own mother had not been able to because of needing to work full time. I hadn't grown up around young children or babysitting and wouldn't ask to hold babies, but I knew holding and caring of my own child one day would be amazing. And it was.

Chapter 2

Sowing High Achievement

M y parents met at an afternoon staff meeting in a middle school library. It was during a school strike in the 1970s. As much as they believed in unions, they each took spit in the face to pay the bills those months. Maybe it was their willingness, or necessity, to work in controversial times that was part of the attraction. My parents joked that she was Lady, and he was Tramp, like from the 1955 Disney movie because their backgrounds were so different. My mother is a white Scandinavian-English American from Minnesota, and my father is a brown Mexican American from Eastern Oregon.

My father, with a fraternal twin sister, was a migrant field worker, who started working at the age of five. As a younger child, he rode in truck beds on days-long journeys with his mother and two older half-brothers. His father was working in other states as a laborer. Their caravan would stop for the night at rest stops along the way. My father remembers that the children slept under picnic tables en route from Southern Texas to farms in Oregon, Idaho, Washington, and Montana.

My grandfather, a native of the central state of Guanajuato, Mexico, also worked in agriculture. When he met my grandmother in the mid-1950s in the border towns of Eagle Pass, Texas, and Piedras Negras, Mexico, he worked legally in the United States through the Bracero Program. He came from meager means and a family of seven. His father died when he was about eight and because of the loss of a stable income, he and his siblings were distributed out to extended family. My grandfather had little to no formal education and possibly struggled with learning differences; however, he made a life for himself thanks to

US work documents that belonged to a deceased first cousin, only a few years his senior.

My grandmother's family was from the town of Allende, in the state of Coahuila in northern Mexico. Her family prided themselves on having risen to the middleclass, and family members worked as teachers, bankers, and doctors. My grandmother's sister took violin lessons, and my grandmother completed school through the eighth grade. She enjoyed reading and writing poetry, drama and singing. My grandmother married young, as was the custom; however, after having two sons, she returned to her father's home as a single mother of two. She worked as a secretary in a doctor's office in Eagle Pass during the day and traveled back to Piedras Negras at night on a work visa. When my grandparents met, all those years ago, passing back and forth over the border, their unique circumstances—she a single mother and he a Bracero worker with a mysterious past—didn't keep them from getting together.

Due to the economics of the times, my grandfather worked multiple jobs in Nyssa, Oregon, an agricultural town where my father's family settled when he was five. The migrant field worker community was growing along with their family. From a young age, my father and his twin sister made bottles, changed diapers as well as fed and bathed their subsequent siblings. A little older, he and his twin also helped clean the house and helped with the laundry. My father's siblings would number twelve by the time he was recruited to a four-year state college at nineteen.

As one of the oldest and darkest skinned of the family, behavioral expectations were set high for my father. Per the era, corporal punishment was acceptable, expected even, from parents and teachers alike. When good behavior was not performed, a strike to the head with a hand, paired with an insult, like "burro," or to the body with a leather belt was the consequence.

One cool morning, among rows of green leafy potato plants, the smell of damp alfalfa in the air, such a strike landed on my father. It was one of his first days working his own row in the fields. After a few paces, he was making mistakes. He didn't clear the row correctly after plunging his hands into the damp ground to retrieve clods of potatoes before putting them in the gunny sack that hung between his jean-covered legs from two large metal hooks fastened to a leather belt he wore cinched tight for his smaller size. No real instructions had been given as he put his potato belt on in the early light of morning, but mistakes cost money. So he was hit, out of nowhere, across the back of his head. I imagine he never made that mistake again.

My father adapted himself in the fields and the classroom to fit the dominant cultural expectations of success. On the first day of school, his name was anglicized to suit the white teachers, and kids were punished if they spoke Spanish. There was little patience for not speaking English well or fast enough. Like my grandfather, and later myself to some degree, my father also struggled with learning to read and write. Over time, he internalized the negative opinions of others—the times he'd been told he was a stupid "burro" and didn't try hard. He hoped to graduate from high school, get a job at the local sugar factory, and get married. However, my grandfather had another plan for my father.

After coming home from track practice sweaty one spring afternoon, my father met a university recruiter. He'd come to the area looking to talk to families like my father's about college opportunities. As was the custom in the family, my grandfather made the decision for my father and told him he'd be going to the state school. Up to that point, all the money my father had ever earned by working in the fields after school or in the summer or later as a forest fire fighter along with his brothers and my grandfather went to the family. With college now in his future, the family bought my father a car, two new green suitcases, and a Parker pen set. The recruiter assured financial and academic support through the Education Opportunities Program they represented at Oregon State University. Once on campus, my father began navigating a broader white American world and explored some of his heritage. He participated in Chicano events and was Chicano Student Union president. My father thought of himself as a cultural chameleon. When he went back home, his Latino identity came out, and when working as one of the few brown employees in the whole school district, he knew he needed to act in ways that did not draw negative attention to himself.

My mother was from a middleclass family who lived in an affluent Minnesota neighborhood with broad green yards extending from Georgian colonial-style homes. Her mother graduated from high school and was an avid reader. My grandmother's parents came from modest means; her father was a printer, and her mother was a housewife. My great-grandparents married for love versus social status. My mother's father was a second-generation Swedish American and an inventor and attorney. Rare for the times, his younger sister attended a university and completed a journalism degree. My grandparents celebrated their wedding a week after the bombing of Pearl Harbor in 1941. Their happy day turned solemn knowing that my grandfather would be needed in the war. Due to his education, my grandfather served in the US Army as a meteorologist in Gander, Newfoundland. With her husband away, my grandmother lived with her parents. My curly redheaded mother was six months old when she first met her father, who would become a source of tension for her family, unbeknownst to her.

Similar to my father, high expectations were assumed of my mother during her childhood. That was likely due to the fact that she was a girl. It seems my grandfather was jealous of her and the attention my grandmother gave her. His own Swedish mother had been the principal caregiver of her eight siblings because their father was an alcoholic, and she had little mothering warmth left in her by the time my grandfather was born. My grandfather would yell at my mother and sometimes at her two younger brothers with little provocation. He craved attention from his wife and didn't like to share it with my mother and her siblings. It seems he had narcissistic personality disorder. As an escape, books were my mother's dear friends from a young age. She once told me that she still had her childhood library card number memorized. Although the relationship with her father was mediocre at most, he did support my mother's desire to attend university. She'd have to pay her own way and live at home. Dentistry was what my mother told me one day was what she really wanted to study. When she approached her father about it, he said, "There are no female dentists," and she took his word for it. As much as she wanted a degree in history or social studies, her male guidance counselor told her to forget about it and that "Those jobs go to coaches," in other words to men only. Title IX athletics didn't exist yet. My mother instead majored in literature because in the mid-1960s, women were either teachers or secretaries.

At the afternoon staff meeting when my parents first met, my mother was already a mother. Her first marriage had ended due to many things, including her ex's alcoholism. My mother left Minnesota and drove out west to Oregon, via a blizzard in Montana, with her adopted Vietnamese daughter, who was then four years old, and fifty dollars to her name. On her first date with my father, she broke down and cried in her side salad at a modest restaurant chain, the kind with framed cross-stitched images of farms and watercolor prints of hunted game. Both my parents' childhoods possessed individual struggles and complex parental relationships or the lack of them. I guess she hadn't talked with someone who was such a good listener, like my father, in a long time. Their cultural differences and childhoods, which were at different ends of the socioeconomic scale, didn't keep them from becoming friends. These factors would shape my parents and how they would parent.

I was a miracle baby and born in the fall of 1983. During my mother's first marriage, she couldn't get pregnant. After tests on her and her then husband of almost twelve years, doctors told them kids were not possible. They completed and successfully passed the rigorous processes of international adoption at the tail end of the Vietnam War. In the spring of 1975, they received my sister, who was five months old. Becoming pregnant didn't seem to be a problem when she was seeing my father some nine years later.

One spring day, in 1983, after a doctor's appointment, my mother told my father her recent health concerns were not due to cancer, as she feared. Her strange symptoms of fatigue, bloating, and nausea were because she was pregnant. She was sure the technicians at the clinic had mixed up her test results with someone else's and requested the pregnancy be tested again. While they awaited the confirming results, my father told her he was sure she was pregnant or else he was crazy. He went on to tell her he'd been getting queasy and vomiting in the mornings just like when his twin sister was pregnant, and she lived in New Mexico!

Creating their own family, now with two kids, my parents made conscious decisions to parent differently than they'd been raised. At six weeks postpartum, and after complications from an emergency cesarean of my birth, my mother went back to work her full-time teaching job. It was my father who continued to care for me because he could not get a full-time teaching job. During my mother's unexpected week at the hospital, days after I was born, my father cared for me at home with my then third-grade sister, and his mother-in-law who'd come to help, but got sick once she arrived. Early in her postpartum time, my mother had a unique opportunity to complete her master's degree at a discount, which she had already started when she became pregnant. So my father provided significant childcare to me while she worked and completed her additional degree before I went to kindergarten at age five.

I don't recall knowing any other families whose father did the amount and quality of caregiving and housekeeping as mine did. Eugene, Oregon, in the 1980s was devoid of much ethnic diversity. My own household was the most diverse, I'm sure. My family was different. With the lack of community diversity, my Vietnamese sister found traversing her teen years to be especially difficult.

She was one of a few Asian students at our neighborhood high school. Since sixth grade, she had excelled in studying Japanese. In high school, she traveled across town, by taxi, paid by the school district, to another high school with a more advanced Japanese language program. In her tenth-grade year, she completed a three-month foreign exchange to Tokyo, Japan. I was a kindergartener. I remember her absence. For a week, while my mom visited my sister in Japan, I walked into the small brown portable classroom that was my kindergarten room and asked my teacher, Ms. Kelly, if she would kindly redo the hairdo my father had attempted. One time while my father was on the phone to my mother, I overheard him say, "Yeah we're good, and Emily's hair looks like a broom with a barrette stuck in it."

My sister's experience in Japan as a tenth grader was so successful she enrolled in another exchange that lasted most of her last year of high school. However, between these exchange experiences, I heard arguing between my sister and my mother, something that I was unaccustomed to. Teenage stuff, I'm sure, but as a five-year-old the unfamiliar tone and volume of shouting made my body shudder, even freeze at times. During one such verbal exchange, I was rendered motionless in the hallway. It was the first loud argument I can remember. Seeing my sister and mother argue that day stopped me in my tracks. The brown and cream-colored Mexican tile of our front entry was cold under my feet, which were stuck in place. I held my breath in shock. The volume of their argument hurt my body. I wanted to cover my ears but couldn't move. In that instant, I vowed to never provoke that kind of noise and tone from my mother, no matter the cost. As a result, an internal dialog started: *Do it how they like it. Right. Don't upset them.*

I felt my sister's second absence to Japan to my core. I cried hard and inconsolably at bedtime for her. I called out, screaming, "I want sister!" I pounded my hands and feet on my bed. With each thud of my pounding, the white fabric canopy that covered my bed would shake to the rhythm. At the foot of my bed, my parents, who'd tried to console me, stood side by side, hugging each other and looking at me with sad faces. Distraught and young, I tried to piece together why my sister was gone. At age seven or eight, I believed that my sister had been sent away to Japan because of something she'd done. I desperately patched together a narrative: *Why else would she leave and not come home to visit me? And when she was home, she and mom argued. She must have made mom really mad.* I didn't want that to happen to me. Being a good kid and not calling negative attention to myself became my subconscious childhood goal. There had been a few instances when my father's voice was raised, and it rendered me compliant so it would stop. Most of the time as a child, I recall our house was as calm and quiet as a library.

I remember the overcast November day when my first middle-school report card arrived in the mail. I was pretty sure I had done well, but seeing would be believing. The crisp white envelope gleamed in the dim afternoon light. Tearing open the seal, I pulled out the folded paper. After my first quarter of sixth grade, I had mostly A's and a B+. I was excited! My father was in the kitchen, too, and I handed him the off-white paper. As he read it, tears welled up in his eyes. He said, "You're one smart kid!" and opened his arms for a big hug. As he held me in his broad embrace, the masculine smell of aftershave wafted from his cheek, and a seed of desire to get more good grades was planted in my heart.

Seeing him be moved to tears about my grades made me feel like I could soothe something from his past. He'd struggled academically in school. The language was different. At one point, he was put into special education classes for not being proficient enough in English and other subjects. My father was getting more education than his father ever had, so there was no support at home for schoolwork. Food was also scarce at home some months. Hunger didn't bode well for learning; neither did navigating a majority culture social structure. When the pantry ran low, he was sent to go fishing for catfish in the Snake River just blocks east of his home. With that association to fishing, I later understood why we never fished. And consequences, at school and at home, were rough. Speaking Spanish at school was an invitation for a ruler to sting the backs of your hands and sometimes leave bloody knuckles.

I was determined to make my father proud of me by my academic achievements, and of himself, with every report card. With each passing year in school, his predicable wet eyes watered the sprouted seed and fueled many late nights of challenging homework in high school. I took on extra assignments my tenth-grade year to be sure to get an A in my global literature class. I'm sure I could have gotten a similarly proud response from my father had I gotten some B's or even a C, but it never happened. I had kept it up so long; I told myself I had to finish high school with A's. Being a top-grade student had become a significant part of my teen identity. I also thought of my paternal grandparents who worked so hard and my paternal grandfather who used an X to sign his name. I also got good grades for them.

These childhood pressures, which I amplified, did not go unnoticed by my body. Starting in grade eleven, my digestion would stop completely for days or weeks. As a result of this internalized pressure to be good in life—paired with detectable intestinal yeast, bacteria, and parasites from memorable summer trips abroad with my parents—my physical and mental health plummeted. From the ages of seventeen to twenty-four, I traveled on planes and by car to see doctors and experts to alleviate my persistent symptoms of fatigue, mood swings, water retention, and indigestion. My menstrual cycle stopped for almost a full year; my health was so poor.

My first year in college, I had to use a separate refrigerator than my housemates to store my food to avoid cross contamination. During my second year, I lived by myself in a mother-in-law styled apartment, blocks from the university my father attended. It was a great space, complete with a phone-booth-sized shower, in which I couldn't bend down in to shave my legs. Monitoring my diet, and taking strong liver-toxic medications at times, set my young adulthood on a very alternative track. I studied and went home. I hardly dated. I had just enough friends; I met a few people from my classes, had my friends from childhood, and made new acquaintances from being an exchange student in Argentina. Because of my health issues, I didn't join in post final exam celebrations at the local bar for pizzas and beers.

Luke and I first met accidentally at a local ski mountain in January 2008. We then met again at a yoga class his mother was teaching and then surprisingly at a neighborhood breakfast spot the next month. That day after breakfast, he finally asked me for my phone number. I was in graduate school, and twenty-four, and he had finished graduate school in acupuncture the year before, at twenty-seven. On our first date, a lunch at a park, he commented, "I love the way you eat," referring to the lean protein and greens I'd packed myself. My lunch sat on my lap in an unfolded sapphire blue tea towel I'd wrapped the container in. I was surprised at his comment—at the fact that he noticed what I ate. I had been on dates, but the health quality of my food was never noticed; they'd just talked about themselves. The weekend before, I had given myself a pep talk in the bathroom mirror: "Being you, without censorship, is worth the chance of being alone." I had negligible romantic relationships, mostly due to my health, but when I had hung out with guys, I noticed I wasn't showing my true colors for fear that they'd move on, in part because of my dietary needs and a reportedly "intense" personality. Luke was different. He loved it all.

During the six years Luke and I were together before I got pregnant with Corazón, everything seemed carefree. We went on meditation retreats. I graduated with a master's in communication disorders, and sciences to become a speech-language pathologist, and in 2009, I started working with Spanish-speaking children with disabilities and their families. In 2010, we got married standing in the middle of concentric circles of our seated friends and family. We traveled, like the time we went to Peru and hiked the Inca Trail in 2012. We both enjoyed trying new recipes in our fourth-story apartment and cleaning up afterwards. We folded laundry and watched television. Anything we did together was truly enjoyable.

Fast forwards to fifteen months postpartum and four months after I had stopped nursing Corazón—I hit my first rough patch as a mother. Corazón and I had been away from Luke for fifteen days on a trip with my parents to visit my sister in Switzerland. Our reentry to being a family of three again was almost the beginning of the end of my marriage. I had solo parented often in Corazón's first year, nursing exclusively, a bit neurotically, and navigated Luke's work/book writing schedule. Now back together as a family, he and I were not connecting or communicating effectively. Corazón and I had an established rhythm, a flow. She was growing and changing so quickly, and I was accustomed to adapting to those changes. Luke would try to engage with her but in outdated ways, and it annoyed me. *Did he not notice she had moved on past that kind of play? Couldn't he see she liked a new food or wanted her milk in the cup with a dog-shaped cover and not the other cup?* I thought to myself.

I was mad in new ways. I burned with a new feeling, red anger, for the first time. I quickly made the connection between my bristly mood and the recent return of my monthly cycle. I took my return cycle as a cue and began regular acupuncture treatments with a woman in town. Her treatment space was in the lovely airy daylight basement of her house. The wood flute music she had playing was a nurturing backdrop to restful sessions. She and I worked together to regulate my hormones, which regulated my mood. After a few treatments, I was feeling like my calm, kind self, again. That summer, Corazón, fourteen months old, helped me get back to enjoying motherhood. It was important to me to be happy as a mother. Happy mothers were good mothers.

Luke and I are both sensitive people. Corazón didn't fall far from the tree. At eighteen months, her personality really emerged. She was bilingual and responded more in Spanish than English. Like me, she gravitated towards creative play with dance, art, and puppets. Her special cuddle things were shirts of mine versus a doll or a stuffed animal. She was our resident poet, making observations about plane contrails, saying one day, "abu [avión] painting cielo." She traveled to five countries before she was two and a half. Curious about everything, she had equally big feelings and upsets. That felt familiar. As a child, I too was known for my full spectrum of feelings.

I don't have many specific childhood memories of my tantrums, but I do recall a sense of loneliness and confusion with my myriad of emotions. I learned to modify my behavior. I skillfully created situations where I wasn't sent to my room to cry and be alone with my upset of sadness, frustration, or anger. For example, I kept things neat and did what was asked of me promptly a lot of the time. I learned to please people and keep them happy with me. In retrospect, I went numb. As a mother, my responses to Corazón and her increasingly frequent expressions of herself were calm and understanding. I labeled her feelings and coached her on how she might feel them healthily, like sit and cry a little bit when sad and frustrated with me by her side. When she turned two, Luke and I started trying to get pregnant again. I wanted my kids spaced out three years apart. It took some time, again, but by November of 2016, I was pregnant. As the weeks went on, I had less and less energy for Corazón's wide range of emotions.

As if hearing fingernails on a chalkboard, my daughter's requests began to physically hurt me. The wane and eventual tanking of my patience and empathy shocked me. It had not always been that way. Corazón's reactions to not getting her way or getting my attention quickly became intolerable. I resented her. One grey morning in late October, I heard myself saying loudly, "God damn it, can you just STOP with the waterworks and whining?!" She looked at me with her big brown eyes, shocked. I thought to myself perplexed, *Who was that? Why are her big emotions bothering me"* My responses to her the last couple of weeks had been less than kind at times, and inquiry was needed. "Jealous," popped into my head, and an acknowledging sense of truth flowered in my diaphragm. Yes, I was jealous of Corazón's emotional expressive freedom and was also newly pregnant. Saying this to myself was like turning on a high-wattage light bulb in a dark room. It blinded me with its brilliance of truth. I had had big feelings as a little kid, yet I didn't have the same permission or space held for me to express them. In the mid-1980s, best-parenting practices regarding feelings and emotions directed parents to distract kids when upset; they said things like "You don't have to cry; you're fine" or "Being angry is an ugly feeling; you don't feel like that." The kids were then sent to their rooms to have their meltdowns in private. My parents followed the advice of the times. That was a huge difference between my daughter's and my childhoods. The bigger the space held, the bigger the feelings expressed.

Some of my earliest memories included one of my nicknames: PD. It stood for "pretty darn." I was said to be either "pretty darn sad" or "pretty darn happy" at any given moment. My family said it as a term of endearment; however, as I thought back on it at thirty-three, it felt more like shame in sheep's clothing. Something inside me felt made fun of, belittled. What was wrong with having lots of feelings? Identifying with my jealousy was a glimpse into an unknown part of myself, like catching a view of your full backside in a three-way mirror. That was my baggage. Those were parts of myself that had been isolated and annexed into my subconscious until now. It was not until my irritation with Corazón rose to a particular volume that I realized I had unfinished business with my own childhood and with my lack of emotional freedom. Being a parent had deeper angles to it than I'd thought. It was so unexpected. Motherhood was not always smiles and happy faces, like the ones I'd seen in family albums or in pictures framed in hallways.

As my second pregnancy continued, my toxic reactions were becoming habitual. Without self-reflective examination, I believed they would become part of our family culture. That was not how I wanted to parent Corazón or behave while pregnant. In an effort to change my own behavior, I stepped into my professional expertise and identity. I made visuals about different feelings with colored paper and stuck them to the side of the refrigerator. I reasoned that we would learn together about all the shades of feelings people have. We would learn their names and feel them, without shame. In my family growing up, my parents took pride in the idea of "doing it differently" regarding their parenting and their ability to achieve it. For example, my father didn't use a belt to hit and punish my sister or me like he'd experienced, and my mother took an in-depth interest in my sister's and my interests, unlike her own mother had done with hers. As parents, Luke and I continued to "do it differently," and changed or ended generational parenting styles or beliefs that didn't align with ours. We didn't spank; instead, we talked and taught about feelings, provided dual-language exposure, and communicated about transitions, routines, and expectations with visuals.

I so wanted to get parenting and motherhood just right. Achieving was what I knew and how I self-identified. Some people called me a perfectionist, and maybe I was. I viewed myself as having high standards. I would keep succeeding with two kids. What could stop me?

Chapter 3

We Knew Better

It was a Tuesday afternoon in early July 2017, and I was forty weeks pregnant. I rested on our red couch feeling very big and then had to pee. The day before was my projected due date. It was also the first day of work for the five-week summer session at my job. These were the weeks in the summer when special education services were rendered to children with disabilities and their families in accordance with federal law. Since I had not gone into labor, I had joined my colleague on a home visit with a Spanish-speaking family, the population I served primarily as a bilingual and bicultural clinician. We all laughed often during the session as I awkwardly waddled with my big belly, trying to get and stay comfortable. Resting now on the red couch, I felt the tax of going on that home visit.

I went to pee, relaxed, and let it happen. Then I heard it—a distinct "tinkle tinkle" that had not come out of my urethra. *Was that my waters breaking?* I wondered to myself, excitement building in my chest. I finished peeing and got up to text my friend and doula. In her reply, she said to lie down and then get up again to see if liquid leaked more. So I did. When I stood up, my pants got wet between my legs. "It's happening! It's starting, and it's so different from last time!" I sang aloud to myself, home alone. In the rush of excitement that sprouted throughout my body, I made a plan with the doula and got a hold of Luke to get home. I called my parents and let them know they'd need to get Corazón from preschool and keep her overnight at least. To savor the magic of this eve of becoming a mother of two daughters, I made a quick video for the baby and Corazón on my phone to mark the occasion and treasure the moment.

A few hours later, we were back in the familiar and supportive hospital room, with the same great views of the surrounding hills, glowing in pinks as sunset started. I was excited to meet our second daughter. I expected labor to really get going, since my water broke at home, and she was my second child. Being strep-B positive, it was highly recommended I come straight to the hospital for intravenous antibiotics. We checked to see if Doris, the nurse who'd supported us at Corazón's birth, was on call, but she wasn't. As the sunset shined pinks and then blue-purples in the sky that July evening, I wondered what this birth story would be like.

At a shift change around 7:00 p.m., the on-call OB came in to meet us. I didn't like her at the sight of her unenthused face and less after she talked to us. Since arriving a few hours earlier, no regular contractions had started, even though my water had ruptured. The doctor talked to us about induction with synthetic oxytocin, called Pitocin, with her hands held in front of her. "It was so early in my labor. Was Pitocin really needed? Already? Was that the only option?" I asked, trying to hide my irritation. Luke had brought acupuncture needles and a microcurrent TENS-unit. We would use those and wait on induction. Hearing our response, the doctor turned and left, her face unchanged. Our labor nurse quickly shut the door behind the doctor, turned to us with a savvy look, and confirmed she would help us with our plan. As if in a huddle, we broke formation and got to work getting my labor going.

Wanting to honor the fatigue that set in at my usual bedtime of 9:30 p.m., we paused our efforts to let me sleep. "This is so different," Luke and I kept saying to one another in disbelief as we moved around the quaint room. Hadn't we done this before? Aren't second babies supposed to come more quickly? Over the course of the night, I slept some, got up and danced some, and waddled around some more. Around 2:30 a.m., some regular contractions started, and we got excited. However, an hour later things slowed again and eventually stopped. With all the moving around to get the baby out, I became hungry. I had not eaten anything in over twelve hours because I could vomit, and in the case of an emergency cesarean, I wasn't allowed to eat. As I rolled over from napping, pink and rose dawn light filtered through the windows. A new day dawned before me, and my belly was just as big as it was when I arrived there. *How long would this take?* I mused to myself.

At 8:00 a.m., there was another shift change. Our fabulous labor nurse went home and another, less peppy one showed up. Fortunately, a smiling OB doctor came in and gave the thumbs up to our nipple-TENS-acupuncture efforts and said, "Keep going!" although nothing much was sustaining. She also said, with a wink and a smile, "Yes, have some breakfast," after I asked, in slight desperation, if I could eat. As a steaming stack of flapjacks arrived, the new nurse and nice doctor came to talk to us about induction. It had been almost seventeen hours since my water broke, and I was four centimeters dilated. As much as I'd hoped to repeat my hypnosis birthing techniques, pregnant life with a toddler had not allowed for the rehearsals. I had listened to the affirmations faithfully, though. During the night before, after the hour of progress stopped, our labor nurse informed us of an alternative Pitocin dose rate and schedule, should it be needed later. We shared this preferred dose rate with the new doctor and nurse, and they happily set me up to give it a try. Waiting for the nurse to return with the drip of Pitocin, I took a deep breath and tried to relax and get ready for a new phase of this journey. This was so very different from my time birthing Corazón. I was surprised and let down a little that my second child wasn't coming fast. Was that just an urban legend?

True to its reputation, the first bits of Pitocin got the cream-colored contraction monitor chirping with activity. Luke, our doula, and I smiled, and I kept moving around the cozy room. Little by little, we upped the dose in an attempt to have my body acclimatise to the drug. Tight, fist-sized cramps began to ram themselves squarely in my uterus just below my bellybutton. That's not what it felt like before. With Corazón, it had been all back labor. What was this pain? Breathing more heavily with each step, and moving more like a pacing animal, my smile fell from my face. My gaze narrowed, as I put all my energy into the sights in front of me to bear the pain.

The Pitocin experience was nothing like my first laboring experience, and I hated it. I wanted it to stop. I wanted to stop moaning in pain, real pain. With each crippling contraction, it felt as if someone jabbed the wide end of a baseball bat into my abdomen. I wanted to leave my body to escape the pain. I was trapped in it and so was my baby. Needing some kind of relief from this chemical torture, I tried the bathtub to get comfortable but that ramming kept on. After a few hours with the Pitocin, my cervix still hovered open at around five centimeters. While still in the bathtub trying to endure the Pitocin blows, I ranted to Luke about the pain and why couldn't he do this part. Gripping the side of the white tub with my left hand, I declared, "I want an epidural. I'm done with this pain." To which our doula asked, "Are you sure that's what you want?" Her question made me pause, just as the nurse announced, "The anesthesiologist is here." I froze trying to think in complete sentences.

"She's not ready for an epidural quite yet," my team told the anesthesiologist, who unknown to me, turned and left to attend to another patient.

Could I do this longer? Didn't I want a natural delivery? I had so many doubts floating through my head. *What will my friend doula think of me if I get the epidural? Maybe I can go without it?* But then the pain of the next Pitocin contraction took my breath away. I rallied through the pain and produced the short phrases "I want an epidural. I'm done suffering."

Forty-five long minutes later, because the anesthesiologist had gone to another patient, I was finally resting flat on my back in a daze of relief. As more time passed, and the uterine pain disappeared, I returned to be the happy person I knew myself to be. We waited then while the Pitocin did its work of prying open my cervix because my body was not doing it. In the wake of my panting and pacing, Luke looked shocked and traumatized from seeing his beloved friend and wife moan like a dying animal. It was so unexpected and different from the swaying and humming goddess that was the laboring woman who birthed Corazón. After catching his breath, on the small sleeper bench he'd dozed on, he went for a walk to get some air and settle his nerves.

Over the course of the early afternoon, the contraction monitor showed a line with peaks and troughs on the screen to my right with the readings of the contractions coursing through my body. Unlike my epidural with Corazón, this one was stronger, or worked differently, because my legs were completely numb and out of my control. At the twenty-four-hour mark since my water broke, Luke and I video called Corazón. We wanted to give her a personal update on her baby sister. She looked so grown up on the screen of my phone. I took a screenshot of our faces in the video screen to remember that moment. Her imminent graduation to big sister was hanging in the air like night-blooming jasmine, sweet and dizzily pungent. As we hung up, the nurse came in and checked my progress, ten centimeters and 100 percent effacement. "It's time to start pushing," she said brightly with a smile.

After thirty minutes of pushing and feeling baby Juliet wiggle her own way down and out the birth canal between my pushes, Luke placed her warm wrinkly body upon my chest. I was relieved our use of Pitocin had not caused the need for a cesarean and a reflex switched on. "Roo-roo-roo roo-roo-roo," I chanted rhythmically. The instinctual and familial comforting sounds I used with Corazón, and my father used with me, and my Abuela used with him, spilled from my lips. I was already a mother. I had a clue about what to do with this warm newborn at my chest. *This isn't hard,* I thought. *The body remembers.* The many hours of logged experience with my other daughter as an infant were already serving me seconds into doing it all over again.

With this second child, I had a feeding and sleeping schedule planned out. We were going to make the most of our veteran parenting skills and fold this new person into our family of three seamlessly and professionally. Our first go of it had gone well enough, and when that rough patch happened after weaning, we knew to plan adjustments accordingly. Now we swaddled with confidence. In the bright hospital room, Luke washed and dressed the fresh baby with ease.

To help smooth the transition to big sister for three-year-old Corazón, we planned a birthday party in the hospital room. Two hours after Juliet was born, both our families and daughter arrived to meet the baby. Corazón wore a pink dress for the special occasion and carried shiny balloons. As they passed the baby around and took pictures, we ate cupcakes. The chocolate- and vanilla-frosted cupcake on my plate had an unlit candle in the shape of the number zero on it. The postpartum high I felt last time after birthing the placenta was nowhere in sight. I was exhausted. I was still amazed at my body but also let down by it, too. Pitocin was brutal to me. As soon as the cupcakes were finished, we said our goodbyes. I knew better, we knew better, than to have me spend energy hosting after the birth.

Back home, two days later, Luke left me propped to rest and to nurse

Juliet while he took Corazón swimming for an afternoon. I sat before a spread of fruits, cheese, avocados, and bottles of water. Sitting there, stocked with food in arm's reach, I reveled at the red-haired bundle in my arms. *"My daughter has red locks."* I thought to myself. It was so unexpected. Corazón had thick dark hair and skin slightly darker than mine, but Juliet would be lighter than all of us.

Breastfeeding brought on familiar toe-curling pain upon latching; however, it didn't stress or surprise me. At the two-week baby appointment, the nurse practitioner offered me a clear silicone nipple guard to try after seeing me wince as I latched the baby. Open to not suffer, I put it on right then and there in that feed. A miracle! Feelings of enjoyment bubbled up throughout my body as I nursed Juliet with the shield and without pain. I melted into the rocking chair of the exam room welcoming the relief. Without a hormone high to crash down from, my postpartum hormones yielded no remarkable fluctuations in my early postpartum as days turned to weeks. The steep, screeching plummet into reality that happened three years earlier on day ten postpartum with Corazón—when Luke had to take her downstairs away from me—stayed a memory of the past. This time, at one-month postpartum, we were succeeding. Growing to a family of four was going smoothly.

In measured chunks of three hours, I woke easily, and without an alarm, gracefully adhering to the prescribed feeding schedule. I remember a night, one of our first back home, when I crept to the wicker basket, a few steps away from our bed. I gently picked up our little peanut of a baby. Juliet, with her head of red fuzz, was just starting to stir, her eyes still closed. That night, I made no big fuss with Juliet during the nighttime feed. I knew better than to turn on lights or change a diaper unless necessary; less effort meant more sleeping. That would become the night routine. One month became two, and I was in awe that my body was relaxed and my nervous system was calm, considering I was waking up every three hours at night. *I was made for this*, I thought proudly.

As the car rolled to a stop on the coastal gravel driveway, a few hours drive from Eugene, I completed ten-weeks postpartum. Juliet's namesake's wedding was the reason for the trip. Re-enacting the seamless feeding schedule of home on an unknown lumpy green couch, however, proved to be impossible. Nocturnal hours of unfamiliar crying from

Juliet ensued. Was it the costal climate? Was it the house? My head spun in disorientation as if I'd rode a merry-go-round too fast. I felt profound frustration down into my bones. *I want to sleep!* I shouted in my head. In this new environment, fatigued, I cracked under all the pressure of two kids.

With experience under his belt, Luke jumped into action at those first signs of distress. As the hours ticked by without sleep, he loaded screaming Juliet into the car and went for a drive. I slept as faint colors emerged into the dawning sky. Our previous experience as parents showed up for the win; get sleep however possible. When I woke up a few hours later, he was back, the baby still asleep as well as preschooler Corazón. He handed me a hot drink. The warm paper cup heated my hands. As I savored that feeling, he informed me that he'd found a local wellness clinic and booked me an hour massage. I was speechless. Tears welled up in my eyes. I was grateful, and I felt a little guilty, too. I knew this prompt, thoughtful, and generous response was not likely the norm for most moms. I agreed to go and would enjoy the quiet and relaxation for them, too.

The small clinic was a few blocks away. Each step away from our lodgings felt as if I were untangling myself from the arms and tentacles of an octopus. As the squares of concrete passed underfoot, my tired body felt lighter, more my own, as I approached the house-turned-clinic on the corner. The practitioner was also the receptionist that Saturday. We passed down the sea foam green hallway to the therapy room, where I undressed. The freedom from children and their needs and space surrounded me like a soft bubble. Soothing music played and hummed in the womb space I found myself in. As if in a trance of fatigue, I shrugged off my clothes and got under the covers on the massage table. I melted into the warm preheated surface like butter on toast. The table held me with tenderness. With a soft knock, the practitioner entered, placed her hands confidently on my back, and started to gently rub exhaustion from my body, my being.

Luke officiated the lovely wedding ceremony. On a tall grass studded cliff, our friends wed, and we celebrated among their guests. Corazón played with other kids at the wedding with zeal. An elegant older woman, with white hair pulled back with an antique comb, offered to hold our infant so we could eat dinner. She said she was a "baby whisperer," and she wasn't kidding. Never mind this person being new, our baby was in the arms of an angel. In awe, and relishing the support, Luke and I sat on the edge of the dance floor and took in our experience thus far as parents of two children. We'd managed a bumpy, overstimulating crying situation successfully.

The tiredness I felt the weekend of the wedding faded, and I was keeping up with our new stride of two kids comfortably. Soon, my job was on my mental radar. Just as I'd gone into labor, two other bilingual team members resigned for personal reasons at the special-education agency where I worked. It was my good fortune and postpartum plan to start back to work at three months postpartum. It felt like the right next step. I was feeling good, and before starting back, we had a family reunion with Luke's family.

Our hopes were high, as the plane landed with a skid and a bounce in Kauai, Hawaii. Luke and I had managed both girls on the six-hour flight from Oregon without any meltdowns. Traveling with two kids was different, and we surrendered to the slower pace. We were intentional about details on the trip, having learned from the wedding weekend. We booked a condo near the airport because our flight arrived right at dinnertime, and after a full day of travel, we didn't want to also drive two more hours to our destination. The round pool, just a few buildings away, and the grounds, studded with palm trees, were a welcoming oasis after being cooped up on a plane all day. Corazón splashed about like a dolphin with Luke while I showed Juliet fragrant plumeria flowers from my hip. The next day, we drove the few hours to the north side of the island to meet up with the reunion. We took our time on the drive and stopped to swim along the way to break up the time in the car. Corazón bobbed around in still clear water wearing the snorkel mask we'd brought with us from home. She was beyond happy, while Juliet played in speckled shade on a blanket.

Our jaws dropped as we drove up the narrow driveway to the modest one-story blue house my in-laws rented with the jungle-green mountains featured in the film *South Pacific* in the distance. Juliet was strapped to my front while Corazón ran ahead and around the large yard bordered by tall palm trees. Beyond them the ocean sparkled, and we saw turtles surfing waves. The views were mesmerizing, especially at sunrise and sunset, with the sky painted in greens and blues and then dotted in pinks and orange. In the first few days, we saw different birds and found shells of all sizes. The girls enjoyed the fresh air, and Corazón splashed in aqua-blue water with her grandmother, uncle, and aunt, Luke's sister. It was beyond beautiful. Although we were in paradise, as the hours and days passed, the confining size of the rental began a slow compression. The whole family of five managed to squeeze into a two-bedroom house, shuffling around one another at times. Then, after two days, the weather changed dramatically.

Rip tides marked the beaches with large chevron arrows out to sea, and swimming was out-of-the-question dangerous. We hadn't planned on there being no swimming options for Corazón or ourselves. The stormy weather meant no big spaces to run and play in and no swimming. Our tenacious Corazón lost her mind with boredom. The activities left over from the plane only engaged her so many times and for so long. She almost literally started crawling the walls. If that wasn't bad enough, Juliet started to practice rolling over and woke herself, and me, up every forty-five minutes at night in the makeshift bed we arranged for her in a closet in our room. Not long before we left for Kauai, I had started supplemental feedings because I wasn't making enough milk. We used a goat-based formula, as it seemed Juliet's system was sensitive to cow-dairy formula. Luke and I mixed and cleaned bottles multiple times a day. It was frustrating because we had hoped Luke's brother or sister might have offered to help us, but they didn't. No one did, really.

Navigating familial relationships that postpartum was different than when we had just the one kid. With a second child, the greater family acted like we had it covered. With one child we had felt very competent as parents. Adding another child to the family was proving to not be as simple as one child + one child. It felt more like one child + one hundred children. I assumed people could see I needed help. Wasn't it obvious? I felt invisible. Instead of asking for help, I just pushed on and stuffed my resentment down deeper inside. As the weather continued to be poor, my resentment mounted just like the dark clouds outside. In response, the other adults occupied themselves with work or other activities, leaving Luke and me, and sometimes my mother-in-law, as the only adults on duty. The functioning ratio of adults to children was three to two or two to two, nothing like the big helpful family we'd imagined. As the reunion wore on, it wore us out.

Since they were my in-laws, I didn't believe I was positioned, or allowed, to voice my resentments at all. We were in a beautiful location, and I didn't want to sound ungrateful or unaware of their generosity. It was against my upbringing and being a good daughter-in-law. However, my body couldn't lie. I stomped around, not smiling much, and as if I were a skunk, the other adults retreated from me. After a particularly pouty morning, Luke and I had it out.

"This is not the family reunion I agreed to come on!" I yelled. He agreed but said I needed to adjust my attitude.

"You're complaining in paradise!" he threw back to me.

I couldn't help it. As if personifying the volcanic environment of the island, and hearing his reply, I lit into a rage. Throwing my clothes that were lying about the bed, I began to rant about all the things that were not what we expected: cold weather, dangerous ocean currents, and adults busying themselves instead of taking an interest in our family or helping us; there was not a single offer to feed the baby a bottle or even hold her. It was all too much, even in paradise. I was breathless after listing my grievances. I felt better though. Keeping quiet hadn't served me any. After hearing it spelled out, Luke agreed: It had been hell in paradise. Then, he sighed so long his shoulders rounded with the weight of it all. We looked at each other and stood to embrace. Together, we decided to not go with the flow of the group but made plans that suited our young family. We were in paradise after all; we were going to have a good time damn it.

In the last two days of our weeklong trip, the weather cleared. We also drove two hours across the island to swim in protected, calm waters. That area of the island was touristy and my husband's family didn't like touristy places, so it had not been considered a choice sooner. We paid to park and lugged our kids and beach gear to a small free space of sand among people and their children playing. I exhaled with relief. I felt my body relax as small kids played in the lapping warm waves.

I went snorkeling alone, the only thing I wanted to do at a minimum on the trip. While Corazón was busy nearby with a new friend and Luke watched sleeping Juliet tucked in the shade of her car seat canopy, I waded into the warm water. The briny liquid held me and washed away the stress of the week like a huge Epsom salts bath. With my black snorkel mask on and face in the water, the sounds of being under water brought me into the present moment along with the yellow-colored fish swimming just below the surface. I took gentle strokes and glanced at all types of fish. Peace at last. I soaked up the quiet underwater world where no one talked or cried, and I just bobbed along. And then bobbed some more.

Stumbling in the small breaking surf trying to stand, I laughed out loud at myself. I turned back towards our blanket and walked along the beach. Luke looked surprised to see me and said, "That's it? You were gone for ten minutes!" in confusion.

"Yep. I'm okay if that's all I get to do. I just needed ten minutes," I replied, deeply relaxed.

Looking at me, and with a compassionate apologetic look, he said, "I'm really sorry we didn't come here sooner. I'm sorry I didn't hear you earlier. As much as I'm not a fan of touristy places, this is where a family needs to be, where things are predictable and family friendly." He said it. We'd have to adjust our life to the unexpected need for tourist spots for a while.

So much had been different with the birth and delivery of Juliet; it was clear we were in new territory with two kids. Luke and I had used our experience in some situations those first four months and had also been surprised by the unexpected, too. At the end of the day, we'd been a team, and I trusted that. Looking ahead to my return to work, I was optimistic that he and I would keep using what we knew and learn as we continued encountering the undulating learning curve that was having two kids.

Chapter 4

A Worked-Over Mother

The Monday after the family reunion, my maternity leave was over, and I went back to work. I was almost four months postpartum. My job, and the familiar pace of work, wrapped around me like a warm blanket. With this pregnancy, my plan was to return to work sooner than I had with Corazón because with her, I had gotten antsy at home doing so much caregiving.

It was early November, and the agency was entering the busiest month of finding children in our community, evaluating them, and determining if they qualified for early intervention or early childhood special education services. It was an "all hands on deck" season. That was my ninth year of a census month, and I knew the drill. Plus, my bilingual speech-language pathology team was two members smaller than it had been just months earlier when my water broke at home. I was a hard worker, and my work ethic was deeply rooted in immigrant grit and assimilation. A familiar voice in my head was encouraging me to not let my team down. Diving into work was all I knew.

With my long tenure at the agency, I remembered the days when there was only myself and one other bilingual speech-language pathologist for our county. That meant two professionals for four hundred square miles. We lived in the fourth-largest county in Oregon. My current caseload was capped due to just having had a baby. I was grateful for the unique opportunity at the agency that differed from other state-funded occupations in the US that had stricter maternity leave policies. I was back to a thirty-six hour workweek, as I had been after my first baby, and was grateful we could manage that financially.

Working this number of hours left room for me to get weekly acupuncture on Fridays.

I had my regular treatments on a padded massage table in a small light-pink treatment room. It was a room with a large window at Luke's own office. My practitioner was following a postpartum protocol to replenish a mother's body. As the weeks went on and autumn rolled into winter, I noticed a pattern emerge. By the end of each week, I was tired from the business of family life and work life. Lying down and face up, with needles in various parts of my body, seemed to release pent-up stress. I imagined pin-prick-sized pressure valves letting out tension, a little at a time. Like clockwork, the day after my treatments I had emotional meltdowns of various sizes with crying and sometimes irritability. Using acupuncture earlier in my postpartum period with Juliet, I thought I would recover sooner. Although I had attended to all the known external needs to make life as a mother of two smooth, these weekly sessions slowly unmasked deeper emotions. I entered a rough patch so much sooner with this postpartum than I had with Corazón's.

At first, the meltdowns seemed related to my impending menstrual cycle. What originally seemed like an extra bad day, with instances of raising my voice to a yell and slamming doors, repeated weekly. And I had begun to notice an additional symptom: skin-crawling irritability with a dollop of rage. Overnight, I had no patience for life, let alone Corazón, who was in the throes of adjusting to big sisterhood and fully in the threes. Her preference for, and attachment to, me had not changed, but it did intensify with the arrival of her sister. Her needs, plus the natural and anticipated needs of the baby, paired with the demands at work, overwhelmed me. Luke and I assumed these were stress-releasing moments. Getting outside, away from the family, and taking some time with, and for myself in nature, did the trick. After forty-five minutes to an hour, I was back to my calm and kind self. "No problem. We've got this," we said to each other.

The winter holidays came and with them fun memories of our girls giggling together as sisters and Juliet exploring shiny wrapping paper. Episodes of feeling dizzied by unending responsibilities at home, plus at work, knotted together. They left me wrung out and became less frequent but more intense. Now monthly, or every eight weeks, I would physically wilt with a growing sense of being overwhelmed. My arms would feel too heavy to have on my body, and my bones felt tired when I laid down to sleep. I believed it was a new kind of PMS with my monthly cycle that had returned at four-months postpartum because my milk dried up. My energy tank was empty, and I eked through the weekends with my family on fumes. I entered my sixth and seventh months postpartum, and the fatigue didn't let up. I wanted the days to be longer so there was enough time to really rest before slogging through all the many parts of life as a working mother of two.

One February day in 2018, I stared at the bleak grey sky from Juliet's bedroom window while changing her diaper and started to cry. Big wet tears welled up in my eyes and dropped on her and the changing pad, leaving large circles of moisture. As I reached for another baby wipe, I tried to keep playing along with the dress-up game Corazón was directing from the grey glider chair next to us. Luke was out of town working for the weekend, again, and I started to fall apart emotionally. I was so, so tired. Corazón wasn't napping any more, and we had our "special Mama time" when Juliet napped. There were no breaks, and I needed one for a whole day. I thought about calling my parents but hesitated. *I had two kids because I wanted them. I should be able to care for them now. I need to get it together. I need to get it together,* I repeated over and over in my head as if my sanity depended on it.

Some weekends, I did call my parents when my husband was out of town. When I didn't call them, I took deep breaths and made plans to get out of the house to pass the time. I willed myself to endure the day alone with them sometimes. Two kids were proving to be so much work. The distraction of the park or mall helped a little but made me more exhausted. *Was motherhood always a grind? Why are my bones tired? People on social media are relishing all of motherhood, what's wrong with me?* I sincerely asked myself, hands on my knees as I sat down on my bed to catch my breath.

That February day, I started crying, I called my parents and asked them to come over. I began to melt down in a new way. After they arrived, between sobs, I told them I needed a break for the day. With confused and worried looks between them, they loaded the girls into their car and drove away. Taking a deep sigh of relief, not realizing I'd been holding my breath for what felt like days, I headed to bed and slept for most of the day. After my four-hour dreamless nap and a shower, I felt refreshed. Like a boxer having been tended to in their corner with butterfly Band-Aids and sips of water, I was back at it. Resourced enough to keep it all going a little longer, I got in my car and drove to get my kids.

Once the crying meltdowns happened more than a few times, we noticed a pattern. This whole scenario repeated itself every six weeks until April when I was eight months postpartum.

Luke and I accepted my all-over-the-place moods and tears as normal and natural; however, they were somewhat unexpected that late into my postpartum. Over time, we saw them as what it took to keep up with life as a family with small kids. We accepted that my body and hormones needed time to even out more months into the postpartum period. I was convinced I was past the timeframe for being at risk for any postpartum mental health struggles. Societal expectations chanted in my mind: *Get on with life* and *Bounce back* especially because I was a second-time mother. It was deafening. Would it ever stop?

As a gesture of overdue self-care, I'd made an appointment with a long-time friend, medical intuitive, and reiki master. I was so tired I was the walking dead. Since the beginning of the month, I had caught myself, more than once, nodding off while I drove to or conducted speech-language therapy sessions at work. My body, down to my bone marrow, ached when I woke up in the morning and still ached when I went to bed.

Since Corazón was born, going to work was a welcomed break from the demands of motherhood. My job as a pediatric speech-language pathologist gave me needed mental stimulation; it was an outlet for creativity, service, and socialization with my long-time colleagues. However, almost a year since Juliet was born, work felt like more work. More work to stay awake. More work to breathe. More work to function as a human. Juliet was, in general, a good sleeper. The month before, in March, Luke had slipped and fallen on some wet grass while holding Juliet. In his attempt to protect her as they fell backwards, he held her to his chest tightly. This tight hug broke her ulna and radius bones in her arm as it had been pinned against his clavicle. For three weeks, she thudded around in a bright pink cast while crawling over our wood floors. Nights were the worst. Juliet had fitful sleep trying to rest with a cast and heal her broken bones. With each subsequent night, she thrashed in her crib trying to get comfortable; her heavy cast thudded against the white rails of her crib. Bleary red eyes greeted me in the bathroom mirror, day after day; after awhile, I stopped trying to hide the dark circles with makeup.

Soft early afternoon light filtered into my friend's healing space through the chic gauzy floor-length curtains that hung over each window. Ironically, her office was across the street from the city jail. The hours of healing experiences completed within that room wrapped around me like the gentle hug of a grandmother. I sank quickly into the heated massage table. A softer-than-soft blanket lay over my clothed body; its weigh felt benevolent and reassuring. The sound of brass bowls being struck lightly, mixed with nature sounds, accompanied my restful experience. My friend's hands hovered over my torso, my legs, and my feet. At one instance, she worked near my head for a long while. As she stood there, I wondered to myself: *What was she detecting with her heightened perception of energy?*

Sitting together in stylish green antique chairs after the session, we reviewed what she'd perceived. Her assessment was that I needed rest and lots of it. As she said that and described more of my session, I felt as if I were underwater in a bathtub. She was speaking to me, but I only half heard her, as I was still in a relaxed place of rest. However, my exhausted frame did slump a little in the shoulders with recognition of what she had said. She recognized I needed support and now. Had my body divulged that since I'd stopped breastfeeding back in November I'd been trying to keep irritation and anger from sprouting out of me? Did the, now dormant, tingling anxiety and writhing sense of being overwhelmed appear to her in my aura? I worried she'd seen these embarrassing truths but I was too tired to care. What followed was explicit permission to seek professional mental health support and take pharmaceutical drugs if deemed necessary. I stiffened straighter and thought, *What?!*

As an experiment, I started imagining what help could look like. My mind started dreaming thoughts of time off from work, a nanny to help with the kids, taking long naps, and a full stop break from motherhood. Holding my still cool cup of water, I refocused in on what she was talking about now—mental health support and pharmaceuticals. I knew I was tired, but what mom wasn't? More times than not I felt like a stranger to myself. I was easily triggered: I shouted and stomped around our house every couple of weeks and ended up cleaning up a room or the kitchen in a fury. But, still, I couldn't see myself taking antidepressants. As the wife of a doctor of traditional Chinese medicine and a proponent of natural medicine whenever possible, I realized in that moment I had not been able to see the extent of my physical, emotional, and spiritual depletion for what it was. Luke and I had not seen my postpartum issues for what they were, nor had we utilized the natural and alternative healthcare world, which we knew so well could support us. I was sure a scrip for a pill would not be too hard to come by but was that what I really needed? Were my body and mind trying to get my attention? I believed in that kind of stuff. Still, my highly sensitive body would put me at risk to many, if not all, of the side effects that came with pharmaceutical interventions.

My reiki master friend had been the first to reflect to me the true state of my holistic self. As if cleaning the smudges from a pair of glasses, I started to see the dire state of my physical and emotional selves more clearly. Before clocking another hour at work, I needed to attend to the disarray of my health and my personal life. Dark moments had mixed into my tired meltdowns intermittently since February. I had dark thoughts about maybe not being alive would make things easier but had shoved them aside. Now was my chance to pay attention before things got worse.

Sitting in a daze, back in my car outside the old brick building of the healing space, I did the most logical thing; I called my best friend. I called Luke. In that moment, it seemed that all the times he'd told me he was there for me, he loved me, and would drop everything for me had prepared me for what happened next. With a shaking voice, I asked his receptionist to get him out of a treatment session with a patient. It took all my will to override my training as a good girl and good woman to inconvenience his patient in this moment of need. With tears wetting my face, I told him I needed him. And then, as if opening a floodgate, I gave voice to my deep need for rest, lots of sleep, and a break from mothering and work. The mere naming of the things I needed and had not felt worthy to say out loud because I hadn't wanted to seem needy or selfish left my shoulders relaxed with relief and my mind freed from performing a mental gymnastics routine on repeat. Still on the phone,

I took a conscious deep breath. I felt lighter. It was now mid-afternoon, and Luke said he could be home in forty-five minutes. We quickly planned to meet at home and talk about our next steps for me and for our family.

While Luke wrapped up his workday, I started my engine and drove back to my office to notify my supervisor what was happening. Driving under big tree canopies and along streets with historic homes, I was the most clear-headed I had been since Juliet's birth. I felt surprisingly energized with a touch of anxiety. I texted my supervisor and asked her to meet me in the parking lot. Waiting for her outside our building, I paced and noticed freshly spread bark mulch and the white rhododendrons around the building. My shoulders relaxed. As she approached me, she looked concerned. I said I needed a break from work and was going home early. I briefly explained how tired I was with Juliet's arm healing at night and that I desperately needed to sleep and recuperate. She, a mother herself, agreed, and we planned to meet the next morning once Luke and I had a plan. I was relieved. I felt supported. I wanted to feel more rested and less frustrated with my kids and my life.

Snuggling with Luke on the couch and looking at our home's lovely view of the west hills of Eugene, we made a plan. I would take six weeks of sick leave from my job, plus a month of unpaid leave. Altogether, I would have ten weeks away from my job to work on my health. By dinnertime, we had replies from our post for a nanny on a caregiver website we'd signed up for. The nanny would help with childcare on the days of the week I had been providing childcare for almost four-year-old Corazón and nine-month-old Juliet. By bedtime, it felt as though I could finally exhale. It was going to get better. I was going to get better and replenished. I would not always be bone tired and depleted. I missed the happy mother I'd been when it was just Corazón.

The next morning, while perched on a low wooden stool in my supervisor's office, I learned that my hard-working reputation had prompted the agency director to ask my supervisor: "Does she really need to make the decision today?" I was encouraged to take the rest of the week off and let them know on Monday if a six-week leave of absence was needed. I felt I'd been punched in the gut. By questioning my decision, I felt belittled. For an agency that supports families with children with disabilities, I did not feel supported. To me, the sentiment exacerbated the stark reality of the generational chasm that existed between the director and me—a forty-year age difference. An extended weekend was not going to heal eight months of progressive sleep deprivation, paired with fits of anxiety and crying and depression, because the natural noise of two young children was breaking down my highly sensitive nervous system.

I got so dysregulated from all the noise of life that I felt overwhelmed to the point that my head would swirl with the running list of mom tasks, like feedings and changing diapers, unloading dishes, folding laundry, picking up toys, coordinating with the gardener, tracking monthly milestones, managing the alternative schedule for vaccinations with the pediatricians, swapping out clothes that were too small for the kids and buying new shoes when they'd grown a size in the span of a few months, and remembering how to do my paid job. The decision to take the leave of absence and focus on my health was the first time I had ever put myself, or my family, before my job. Sitting on the low stool, I felt an increasing guilt seep up from within me like water soaking into stocking feet on a wet bathroom floor, slow and cold. I'd made more work for my supportive supervisor to find coverage for my cases and if I stayed any longer, my negative self-talk would get me to waver on my decision. It took all my might to override years, generations even, of being a so-called good girl, a good citizen, and then a good woman. I stood up to leave on shaking legs. My supervisor hugged me and said she would take care of everything. "Feel better," she said. Walking out of the building, I felt like my feet weren't touching the ground.

Chapter 5

Nannies and Negative Self-Talk

More than a year into motherhood with Corazón, and at the age of thirty-one, I had begun regular counseling with my mother. Our relationship had slowly calcified since I was in graduate school and had met Luke. A few months into therapy, I found myself paralyzed with anxiety. I felt unable to tell my mom I might be pregnant again. *She's gonna think the kids are too close in age*, I worried. I also believed that if I were pregnant again, already, it would somehow make me a failure because our plan was to space children out more. (I didn't turn out to be pregnant.)

It was during a session in the wintertime when I mustered the courage to tell her. She was thrilled! In the moment of her elation, I sat tearing up in my chair, and I realized that my negative self-talk had lied to me. Those thoughts, in my mom's voice, were things my mom might have thought of me or not at all. Time stopped in the small blue room with the built-in shelves along one wall, windows facing east, of the repurposed bungalow house turned counseling offices. In an instant, I began to assimilate the reality that what had once sounded like her voice in my head was not her voice but one from within me. I had so many questions.

Later that day, while on a walk with Corazón the volume of that voice amped up. The more I paid attention to the thoughts in my head, the more I heard opinions about everything: what I wore, how I did my hair, complaints about my partner, my abilities at work etc. Sometimes, the voice was so loud it dominated my headspace and made me want to climb out of my body. Deep down, I knew it was not me but a collection of opinions from society and my environments. I reflected that throughout my life, the voice had kept me in good standing with people and at times safe. But it had built up and blocked out my sense of self or my own voice. And now as a new mother, that voice, with its opinions, flooded my mind disguised as my own voice. I needed to sift and pick my way carefully through these thoughts and examine them. Where did they come from? Were there ones I wanted to keep? Did I believe them?

Stopped at a red light on the way home from speaking with my supervisor, I pondered more deeply the reality of us hiring a nanny. Tension seized my gut at the thought. I suddenly felt sick. I personified the feeling and believed it had an opinion, a strong negative one, about hiring help. Thinking about the word "help" created a foul sensation for me. Weak people needed help, lazy people, right? However, instead of shaming myself, I got curious. In the quiet space and time of the drive home, I asked myself, *What's my hang up about hiring a nanny?* While I listened to my body and the thoughts that came to mind, biases bubbled to the surface from my chest and abdomen. The word "movies," flashed in my mind like a bright marquee. *Okay. How were nannies in movies of the late 80s and 90s depicted?* was my next thought. From what I could remember, nannies were depicted working for rich families and for parents who seemed uninterested in their kids or being parents. *That's not me or is it?* I asked myself. Then my negative self-talk joined my mental conversation: *A nanny, really? Aren't nannies for parents who are too busy to show up for their kids? Having a nanny means you can't hack it as a parent and don't want to spend time with or love your kids. Good mothers love spending all their time with their kids. What's the saying? The hours go slowly but the years fly by?*

Whoa! I had never taken the time to listen to my own biases. Listening to this negative narrative reverberate around my cranium made me want to plug my ears. As awful as it was to listen to, it enlightened parts of me to myself. These were my opinions about things that I had never considered. These were unconscious beliefs whose reign was about to end.

When we had only Corazón, I provided the childcare for the two days a week I wasn't working. Luke's work schedule had him working weekends a couple times a month, and I cared for Corazón those days, too, mostly alone. Now, doing caregiving with my reduced work schedule and Luke's unchanged schedule with two kids was not sustainable. Shaking my head as if to shake the volume down on my negative self-talk, I knew what my family needed, and it would happen: more help. I was a good mom for asserting so. My beliefs about nannies were limiting and hurt our family. I overrode feelings of being an inadequate mother for needing childcare.

My body required almost two full weeks of fewer caregiving responsibilities for me to relax enough to sleep when I felt tired. On day fifteen of my leave of absence, I finally took a nap. As tired as I was, I couldn't sleep. During the day, the mental *do, do, and keep doing* drumbeat kept time. Its rhythm shepherded me in line as a mother who did it all. One soothing gift from the universe was an answer to an intention I wrote in mid-April before going to see my reiki master friend. I'd asked for my dream job as a clinical supervisor. Working directly with little people the same ages as my own kids was a bit too much lately; dealing with toddlers at home and at work was oversaturating my senses. I'd always enjoyed hosting graduate students out in the field and dreamed I would be fulfilled supervising. During the first week of my leave, while I tried to slow down and rest, an email from the clinical education director at the local university was in my email inbox. I had been solicited for my dream job! I applied right away. It felt as if the universe had thrown me a life preserver, and I grabbed a hold of it and felt a tender sense of hope. The clinical supervisor job glistened in the distance, and some days I felt warmed with feelings of positivity and possibility. Though most days, without any current work distractions to take my attention, my negative internal narrative crept into my head and took center stage. The voice sounded louder than ever that day: *Be grateful. You need to be respectful. Good people contribute and do their part. You owe them (my parents) something for helping you. Nothing comes for nothing, you know, and why can't you just do this motherhood thing. It's not that hard to do. You have a master's degree for goodness sake!*

The negative self-talk ran nonstop as May passed into June. Sometimes, it left me with a swirling feeling in my chest and feeling completely overwhelmed. That happened one day when I went to my parents' house to pick up Juliet. She'd been with them, rather than at daycare with her sister, due to a fever. Suddenly, a typical diaper change was enough to ignite an emotional bomb. Without observable provocation, I chucked the diaper bag and surprised the baby by yelling a guttural "ahhhhhh," which unleashed Juliet's ear-piercing screaming. My actions as well as the noise made my parents' eyes widen. Their surprise, fear, and discomfort around my anger, rage even, were reflected back to me with expressions of shock and confusion. My heart beat fast, and my skin felt too tight; I ran away to another room to hide, to punish myself. I felt like a child running away to initiate the punishment before it's been given. I felt humiliated for scaring my baby and loosing my shit, my composure. For what?

My negative mental voice scolded me: *Now you've done it; you're a horrible mother! What were you thinking making your baby scream like that? What kind of mother just explodes like that? You should really calm down.*

All the noise was too loud, and all the light in the rooms was too bright. The baby's crying was physically painful, deafening. I had kicked a hornets' nest and was trapped in an angry swarm. Then more guilt and more shame doused me. My voice continued: *Really? You're still upset about this? CALM. DOWN. You're scaring Juliet! Be done. This is not acceptable. You've taken enough attention. You're being dramatic. It's not about you anymore. When will you ever get that it's NEVER about you. You're a MOTHER. Now what did you expect?!*

I tried to rally myself together after that final earful from inside my head. Wiggling my feet down into my parents' plush white carpet to ground and center myself, I breathed in deeply and out long and shoved that noise out of my head. The handful of outbursts like these had been happening in the privacy of my own home that winter, alone with my two kids, or maybe with Luke in the early hours of dawn, but that was the first time my parents saw one. When Juliet started to scream, my mother took her out of the house to the attached garage to get the volume away from me.

At one point, I remember trying to calm down while kneeling on their soft carpet, hands gripping the material to stay as present as possible. Eventually, I went out to face my parents. I was running on fumes and overwhelmed. I wasn't myself. Although my actions had communicated otherwise, all I wanted in that moment was to hold and comfort my scared baby. I was terrified, too, and wanted to be held. As I gathered up the contents of the diaper bag that I'd thrown, the furrowed brows and confused-looking eyes of my father, who'd been frozen in place since my outburst, threw their own punches. I barked at him: "Don't look at me like that!" Whether he consciously registered a feeling of disgust or not, that is what I saw in his eyes. I was disgusted by my behavior. *When would this be over?* I screamed in my head while clenching my teeth.

A few days later, the nanny we found via the online ad came for an interview. Her long hair and smiling face radiated youthful energy. As the nanny shared about her interests and experience, it was evident she was caring, artistic, and open to learning whatever was needed to provide the kind of care we wanted for our children. Before she pulled up in her little white car, I went back and forth in my head over how to train her. We had used babysitters before, but this felt different. We would be the first, in my lineages of families or among our friends, to hire ongoing in-home private childcare. The privilege to do so felt stiff like a starched collar that itched—outdated and humiliating. However, we needed the help, and I got over myself and blazed a new trail of family experiences. I embraced the role and identity of teacher I was familiar with in my professional life and gave her a tour, starting in our open-floor-plan kitchen and living room.

As we walked around our home, I described how I wanted her to offer choices to Juliet and label what she was touching and doing as ways to enhance her vocabulary. My best experiences with kids were logged giving speech-language therapy. Using intervention techniques at home, too, was natural to me. Since we had a bilingual household, I encouraged the nanny to be brave and use whatever Spanish skills she had. The more I declared how I wanted her to interact with Juliet, the more secure in my mothering I felt. I went on to talk about waiting and watching to see how Juliet communicated. That would show when Juliet wanted an activity to continue or to stop. I gave much thought and attention to the kinds of interactions I had with my daughters. By sharing those interactions, I owned them, and it felt good. I was a mother and a therapist, and there was no teasing one out of the other. Seeing the nanny smile, and hearing appreciation from her for the opportunity to learn how I wanted things done, gave me a deep sense of peace. My body eased into the new role of boss. While I showed her where things were, I felt a part of myself muzzling my negative self-talk that was ready to chime in. As if overstuffing a closest with coats and then quickly shutting the door, I felt my mind muffle the words *control freak*. Was I controlling? Maybe, but for good reason: They were my kids. I wanted them well cared for. I wanted their childhood language environment to be optimal because I was insecure about how to be a mother it turned out. I relied heavily on how I'd been trained to give speech and language therapy, as it was the only way I knew how to successfully interact with kids. It was also an attempt to atone for the handful of times I had lost my temper. If I wasn't able to provide a thoughtfully balanced ratio between language-stimulation music and quiet that I envisioned, due to my physical and mental health and otherwise self-deemed inadequacies, then I would ensure that the job would be done well by another caring adult. Saying what I wanted, even though fraught with fear of offending the nanny, felt good. Comfort welled in my chest. The sky did not fall, and she accepted the job.

With the nanny hired and no home or preschool visits for work, I got in my car, twice a week, and drove to my counseling appointments. Walking up the worn wide green steps of the bungalow, the same one I'd gone to years earlier with my mother for our counseling sessions, I slowed down and felt my feet under me. Having her support and the ability to regularly talk to a professional was starting to help me a lot. She was a mother, too. Sharing what was getting me down and frustrated was met with the resonance of personal experience.

Towards the end of my first week, she recommended me a book, *Your Rainforest Mind*. I remember her describing a "rainforest mind" as a trait in which many things are interesting to a person, who appreciates the immense depth of detail, nuance, sensitivity, and emotion of each interest. My counselor told me that the extent to which I thought about the future and the possible effect my actions would have on my kids in their future was a load not all mothers carried. Really? I wanted my kids to get through childhood happy. That would assure me that I'd been a good mother and gotten an A in it. I saw that my changes in mood—starting during my pregnancy with Juliet, and more so as months went on later into my postpartum year—were affecting

Corazón. Was that just how it was? I didn't want to be the source of childhood pain for my kids and then fodder for future counseling. I worried about it.

Since childhood, I have understood myself to be too much or too intense for people, particularly my peers. Play dates when I was a child were often followed by long periods of silence, which made me think I'd done something wrong or said something to not get invited back. I felt not enough, too. In high school, my grandma-aged counselor identified me as having a highly sensitive personality type.

This counselor at the time held a presence of unconditional love. She educated me on myself and taught me to see myself as whole and valuable versus broken and worthless. Discovering my traits of high sensitivity helped with my self-acceptance. I made sense to myself. But since becoming a parent, I had not considered I would be a highly sensitive parent, too.

I shared this with my counselor: "In the moments I'm overwhelmed and frustrated by the requests from Corazón that don't seem to stop, and my head is throbbing from the noise, and I feel dizzy trying to process her words and the task I'm doing, I fear my response will have her going to therapy when she's older." To this, she reminded me: "That's your rainforest mind. Yes, she might go to counseling; however, she is also having quality childhood experiences with you when you follow her interests, for example. Try and notice times you're proud of yourself. Also, what could your frustration, or anger even, be telling you? What are you needing?"

What was I needing? A mother could have needs? It was such a novel concept. A good mother, a good woman, was low maintenance in my head. Didn't having needs make me selfish?

I devoured the rainforest mind book in two days. A lot resonated with me. On the whole, it clarified types of perfectionism: intrinsic and extrinsic. I started to see how I strove for a form of a perfect motherhood, of being a perfect mother, without realizing it. It was a continuation of my high achieving academic childhood. I remembered my high school boyfriend saying, shortly before he broke up with me, "No one wants to be with someone who's perfect!" It landed like a slap across the face.

Before having kids, many people probably took me as a perfectionist. They saw me as a high achiever. The legacy of wanting to make my father proud of me, and himself, grew into extrinsic perfectionism. As time went on in high school, I believed I should keep up the reputation I'd started for myself. It became my identity. As mother to Corazón, I wanted to keep a tidy house because a good mother would, and I struggled to keep that belief viable with Juliet. It took much more effort now. In retrospect, those efforts of perfectionism were synonymous with worthiness. Striving for that kind of perfection wasn't working any more.

As I turned more pages in the book, the examples of intrinsic perfectionism—such as being brought to tears upon hearing beautiful music or working tirelessly to tidy one's living space for the aesthetics—showed me how I longed for an internal perfectionism. I believed and now understood that messiness, figurative or literal, was not valued or acceptable. My father cleaned and tidied often when I was a child. He said that coming from a large and marginalized family, they often lived in chaos and mess, and he hated it; he vowed not to live like that as an adult. My academic striving started as intrinsically motivated perfection and morphed into extrinsic perfection. With time, I appreciated, and began to value, who I was and how I functioned in the world. How could I be a good mother and not be perfect? There were so many unexpected questions about motherhood that it baffled me. In my mind, there were only good-perfect mothers and bad-selfish mothers. Anything in between was still not good, so what type of mother would I be if mothering perfectly was withering me?

Chapter 6

Me and My Mini Me

As if by divine design, weeks after comprehending my jealousy regarding Corazón's freedom to feel intensely and a month into my leave from work, I attended a four-day workshop with seven other women. I heard about the opportunity a few weeks before from Luke. I'd never done group therapy work before. Leaving Eugene to be nestled up against the green foothills in Ashland was a needed escape. The drive through mountain passes and cow-dotted fields was a welcomed change of scenery. Driving fast to keep up with California drivers, at times, reminded me I was alive. I stayed in a modest motel, just off the freeway. Once checked into my room, I reveled in the silence that filled it. I had space to just be. I had space to think complete thoughts and daydream if I so chose. I had the space to sleep. I abandoned my mom duties at the door and felt a bit naked. I would have four days to get to know myself again.

In a hilly neighborhood, just south of a small university, the other participants and I began arriving at the white house where our sessions would be held. It felt like the first day of school. The windows in the kitchen and eating area featured views of the eastern side of the valley. It was breathtaking. As the other women arrived, the electric potential of change and healing was palpable. After some refreshments, we each took our seats, in a circle in the living room. Some chose to sit on the floor on the soft area rug, hugging pillows. I felt the most secure seated on the white loveseat opposing the facilitator. Luke had been studying with him, for the past year. Remembering this settled my insecurities as I got comfortable.

The Jungian-trained facilitator used somatic experience techniques, like guided body awareness, to help us feel into our bodies. Those tools helped us locate where we felt sensations, like tension or heat. These sensations were clues to where we stored unconscious and unprocessed emotions. Each woman there took a turn sharing about her childhood, and my body tensed with shock and deep sadness as people spoke. Intimate accounts of abuse and neglect as well as pressures to perform athletically swirled in and around all of us. It was intense to bear witness to these traumas. Within my head, I debated whether I belonged in that circle or not. I had not experienced unspeakable abuse or neglect. My issues of perfectionism and people pleasing seemed like a nonissue compared to the heinous acts some women there had survived. It was proof that the selves we presented to the world were fractions of, or not anything like, the person and their experiences within. Beholding privileged parts of people, strangers just hours before, rendered us sisters of a chosen kind. By the end of the first day, it felt as if we'd lived decades together. Even though our hurt as girls varied greatly, our longing to feel safe, be seen, and be valued were all the same.

We each took turns working our way deep into dormant feelings and aspects of ourselves. Through completing sentence stems prompted by the facilitator, I looked at things from my past in new ways. I remembered things that I had tried to forget. No judgment was made upon excavated bits of ourselves we'd disassociated from. With each woman's turn, we all experienced various personal breakthroughs. Upon hearing others' struggles with perfectionism and attempts to overcome it, I broke through some of my own internal pain and struggles of why I'd kept trying so hard to be right, good, and perfect. I realized I could stop now. Having the company of those women and the space and time to unpack those parts of my past allowed me to lay them out before myself and analyze what I would keep and what I would trade in for new skills. The increased perspective yielded profound clarity and calm for me.

After lunch on the fourth of five days, the facilitator's wife gave a talk on the concept of one's inner child. My mind lit up with surprise upon hearing that when I did not quite feel like myself in a situation, it was likely due to some other part of me, a younger part, that had shown up. That made so much sense to me. It validated feelings of feeling younger than my actual age. All those times in school, on dates, and while mothering that had easily overwhelmed me were the announced arrival of a younger version of myself. Eyes glued to the silver-haired speaker, I felt into my bodily sensations with a new sense of knowing and curiosity. Realizing that my inner child coexisted in me, as part of me, was like getting a long-awaited vision prescription, and I began to feel and see her. I saw the twelve-year-old girl who wanted a group of girls to like her in the middle-school bathroom and not reject or betray her. I felt the five-year-old girl who did not want to make her parents upset by taking up space with big, and sometimes messy, feelings.

Before I left for the retreat, I shared with Luke how I felt sick to my stomach with the thought of going, even though I thought it was a good idea, and I wanted to go. He'd asked me, "When else in your past did you feel like that?" Middle school came to mind. I was as nervous as a twelve-year-old. My younger self worried, "Would the other women like me?" That was it! I had felt a bodily sensation, used my imagination to tune into the age of myself when I felt it most, and then pinpointed my anxiety: "Would I be liked?" I felt confident, most of the time, as my adult self; however, it was my twelve-year-old self who needed reassurance. Luke's question had been an exercise in befriending my inner child before I even knew that part of myself.

Two days into the retreat, we planned Luke and his brother would bring the girls down to visit me. We wanted the girls to feel supported and connected to me, to the family, as it was a stressful time for them, too. My turbulent moods were uncomfortable at best and traumatizing at worst. Seeing me relaxed and happy was important to us. Given some space from the role of mother, I could feel again how much I enjoyed my kids and missed them, which was a lot. Seeing them again, in the parking lot of the motel, transported me back into a version of mom mode for a few hours. However, with my new self-awareness and perspectives on past motivations for perfection seeking, I was curious about how parenting would now go as I walked out to the car to un-buckle them from their car seats.

Since Juliet's birth, setting boundaries at bedtime with Corazón had become challenging. The transition between coloring at the table and then brushing her teeth was becoming impossible. I could not follow through. Corazón had become an expert negotiator since the time she could put more than three words together, and I had unknowingly encouraged it. It had gone on for months, almost a year now. I frequently got irritated at her during these transitions. Was it typical three-year-old behavior? Was I just bad at setting boundaries and being consistent? It was another piece of my parenting that I wanted to look at, and I just didn't know how or when I would process it.

On their first night, Corazón and I got some time together in the model swimming pool. We splashed and danced in the water. It was so fun! As the bedtime hour approached, I asked her what *last* things she wanted to do before getting out: jump in again or go in the hot tub for a quick warm up. She proceeded to spout an elaborate list of lasts. Before I knew it, another fifteen minutes passed, and we were still in the pool. I tried to transition us out of the pool again, and she defiantly did what I had asked her not to. *Here we go again! How the hell do I get her out of here and not lose my shit?* I thought, trying to seize the ripe opportunity for changing our dynamic. Checking in with my body, I took a deep breath, and I identified my irritation to myself. Next, I imagined how old I was a previous time I felt stuck and not clear-headed, as I did just then. I felt only a half-foot taller than my child in that moment, and I realized my inner child had shown up. She'd heard all the ideas and liked all of them. That was the part of me that didn't want swim time to be over just because it was bedtime. There was no way the younger part of me was going to pass up more playtime with a friend like Corazón. My inner child reminded me, chlorine wafting off my skin, of how I'd longed for friends like my daughter when I was her same age.

Shivering and dripping wet, I said, "Time to get out" in a direct voice. I wanted this transition to go differently. I was upset, but I was not going to raise my voice or yell this time. That was the old pattern. That was not how I wanted to mother. She noticed.

"You're getting mad," she said.

"No. I used a direct voice because I was giving you a direction. I was telling you what I need you to do." That explanation seemed to satisfy her because without a word in protest, she proceeded to get out of the pool and headed upstairs in full cooperation.

Having said goodnight to her and Juliet in their room with Luke and his brother, I walked back to my room thinking, *Wow, that really went well! What were other inner child pieces I've been bypassing?* I needed to sleep on that exchange with Corazón on the pool deck before I understood more. Looking up at the ceiling from bed, the last night of the retreat I tried to remember parenting moments where I had started out with my evidence-based and even-keeled parenting and had ended in frustration and yelling. The majority of these moments had been around topics of limit setting and transitions from a fun activity to something less fun. I knew from my job that transitions were hard for kids, so I used all my therapy techniques to ease them, but more times than I liked, I ended up raising my voice and then felt guilty and ashamed for losing my patience. Good moms were always patient, right? Reflecting more on what happened in the pool, I could now imagine how easily my inner child had come in, engaged with my daughter and lost track of time. It was fun swimming. I'd love it as a kid. When had been the last time I swam around like a mermaid or a narwhal? It was when my adult self, my high-achieving mother self, came back online, realizing it was twenty minutes past bedtime, and the routine had not even started yet that I lost my temper. My negative self-talk message of good kids come from good mothers amplified my perceived failure as a good mother, and I got even more mad at myself. It seemed a part of me, a younger part, had been sabotaging my parenting. Seeing the inner child who had so desperately wanted a friend, and had found one in Corazón, flooded me with compassion. I had a need to play, and if left unmet, it would distract my attempts at setting boundaries.

Gripping the black steering wheel and with a lightness to my mood, I came to a stop at a red light. I was driving home from the retreat. At that light, after taking a deep breath to let the silliness go, I started an audible dialog with my inner child: *Hi... I know you love playing with my daughter. She's so fun and has such creative ideas. From now on, I will make time for more play. You can trust her. She won't betray you or leave you. I will make time for us. I see you and how much you want to play.*

As the light turned green and I turned right onto the overpass above the interstate, a peace enveloped my heart and chest space. There was a relaxed feeling in my abdomen, and I felt ready to parent my two kids as well as my inner child. Clarifying her to myself on the drive home changed my parenting enormously over the next weeks and beyond. Setting boundaries and following through got easier and eventually became second nature. The first couple of days back home I literally held my belly, where I felt my inner child in my body, while I set expectations with Corazón. Understandably, there was pushback and an uptick in boundary testing. Over the course of two to three weeks, each limit I set felt less tumultuous inside myself. My adult self was direct, calm, and consistent. That was the parent I wanted to be. When I joined in drawing with markers, dress up, or diving off the diving board at the community pool with her, I smiled to my inner child self. These were the moments in life when time stopped. That felt liberating. I was happy, and it left me feeling calm and energized.

Chapter 7

The Dark Side of a Mom

O n a sunny June evening, the kind where you can wear shorts and your favorite flip flops, I suddenly became agitated again. I felt dizzy with erratic jitters in my legs and abdomen, and in an instant out of control emotionally. Simple things, like the typical sounds of nine-month-old Juliet, disproportionately annoyed me. They made me cringe, whereas four months earlier, they often enveloped me in awe.

My behavior still seemed strange to me. I didn't want to lash out with a growl or a shout. That had already happened. The urge to run to my room and hide was strong but was lately not an option with Luke's work schedule. Throwing dishtowels with a guttural "Ahhh" or clenching my jaw and fists while stomping away from our girls was becoming common. Would throwing a plate be next? Keeping the monster in our house that looked like me at bay was not easy. Each time these electric sensations showed up, I could not imagine where my irritation and anger were headed, and it scared me. In my worst-case imagination scenario, I would scream, yell, and shake and then leave the girls and not come home.

Feeling a skin-crawling sensation roll down my arms and up from my ankles, I took the cue and put on my athletic shoes. The last times I felt this way I'd slowly morphed into a werewolf of sorts. With swirling aches throughout my body I was no longer patient, kind, and funny. I'd sulk and pout. If you touched me, I might have snarled and shown my teeth. So with my shoes tied, I grabbed the second-hand grey umbrella stroller out of the front closet, strapped Juliet in with no time to waste, and headed out the front door. (Corazón was having an overnight with my parents it so happened. Thank god!)

Headphones in, I cranked up Shakira as I pounded down the hill of our steep street to the flat one below us. I pushed and paced up and down that street for a good forty-five minutes. With each footfall, I imagined I was stomping down the creature of furious fiery rage inside who kept clawing to show up. With each push of the torn black foam handles, I gripped them harder until my knuckles were white. "What the fuck is going on with me?" I said out loud. Who was this woman on a controlled rampage pacing a quite summer street? I then repeated aloud, "This is not what I thought motherhood would be like! Why am I always angry? It's an anger that makes my skin crawl. I clench my fists and want to punch something. Is this rage?"

After two laps along the gold-lit street, I calmed down enough to be tired. I slowed to a stop in front of a quaint yellow house with white shutters and took a long exhale. That's when I looked down into the worn stroller and saw my sweaty, redheaded Juliet asleep. She deserved more than an edgy, crabby mama. I did, too. My body felt itchy and tingly. I walked us home at a calmer pace; Juliet was still slumped over asleep. Once home, I parked the stroller and Juliet to the side of the narrow entryway and decided to let the baby sleep. I then sat down at my laptop to write. I needed to document my bodily and mental experiences to validate myself and to see myself. As a mom of two young kids, I felt alone with my oversized feelings, which seemed to erupt out of nowhere without warning. Seeing my words appear in black type across a fresh Word document served as a personal proof of life.

My body cooled down the more I typed. I felt more like myself again. The evening walk had served its purpose: It actively slowed the anger train before it built momentum. Looking out our window to the surrounding lush green hills of Eugene, I was flooded with the familiar questions: What's going on inside me? Why am I on edge when I have two magical daughters? I'm a repeat mother, not a first timer, so what gives?

At the first two well-baby appointments with Juliet, almost a year earlier in the fall of 2017, I completed a questionnaire about postpartum depression. I sat in a comfortable chair in the windowless waiting room; knee-high kids' toys were to my right, and new moms with week-old babies sat across the aisle. Juliet looked around at the room's blue walls from her portable car seat positioned on the floor next to my feet. I mentally patted my own back in praise as I calculated a score of zero on the Edinburgh Postnatal Scale of Depression. *You're doing it— beating those baby blues—good job!* the voice in my head said. After the three-month checkup, the appointments spaced out, and because most pediatricians assume postpartum mood and anxiety disorders are most likely to start in the first three months postpartum, I didn't get a questionnaire anymore.

Now June 2018, Juliet's birthday a month away, and a month off from work, I wasn't seeing much positive change to my moods. I needed to see my gynecologist. Maybe she could run some tests and get me feeling better. Since moving back to Eugene to complete my under- graduate and masters programs, I'd started seeing my mother's gynecologist. That June my mother had an upcoming mammogram, and being quite the outside-of-the-box problem solver, she suggested I take her appointment. For the previous months, I sensed my parents' concern for me and my mental health but hadn't the ability to talk to them much about it. My mom agreed that getting some lab tests done could be helpful. Upon confirming her mammogram, she confirmed that she also wanted to keep the optional check-in appointment with our physician. Out of desperation, and willing to ask for forgiveness rather than permission, we both showed up to the consultation time. Our doctor was happily surprised to see me until we revealed our intention—that I'd take the appointment and not my mother. Our doctor's face looked concerned, and she kindly and professionally explained that this wasn't the best way to get in to see her, but she'd make it work. Next, she stepped out and got her nurse to create an appointment for me to clean up our unconventional strategy. I felt bad for breaking the rules, but it was my mother's desperate attempt to get me help fast.

While we waited for the doctor to return, I took in the view before me: a standard examination table with its fresh tissue paper cover, a blue disposable pillowcase, and extended stirrups. My mother beside me, I reached for her soft, wrinkled fingers. Her wisdom was a source of support I desperately needed in that moment. The true weight of my shame and burden rendered me speechless and I doubted the small, padded bench would hold us. As the minutes passed, my gaze went up to the ceiling. Dangling over the exam table was a colorful clay fish mobile. As I watched it a spotted red fish slowly turned towards us. Its oversized lips froze in a look of surprise. I was convinced it was already shocked by the words I intended to speak.

As my long-time gynecologist returned, with a look of concern, I confessed: Life as a mother of two was as terrifying as a horror flick. I stared at the floor and offloaded all that I had assumed I needed to carry. I spoke of the sudden and intense mood swings that had erupted at simple requests from Corazón over the past six months, like "I want more cheese" or "Where are my shoes?"

At first, these eruptions had come and gone, like PMS. However, they had ramped up back in April. I was feeling paralyzing, skin-crawling feelings of overwhelm and agitation. These feelings consumed me like a frenzy of sharks. I found myself pacing. I found myself talking to myself in irritation, annoyance, and confusion: *Why do her protests to finish her milk provoke me to feel a boiling sensation throughout my body and I end up yelling?* In some instances in the previous six months, I found myself crying and hitting my calves with both of my fists trying to make the sensations stop. The sound of my yelling and slamming doors would reverberate out to our front porch. It was like I'd turned into a puffer fish or a porcupine. One seemingly small move, comment, or sound and—poof—I'd prickle out and sting those around me with my words or a look. I had developed a negative reflex to everything and anything, and it was all consuming; it controlled me.

On my worst day, a few months back in April, as Corazón was running towards me, I suddenly experienced a flood of rolling tingly heat rise and swell in my chest. It boiled into rage in a way it had never before. "Mommy's not safe. Stay back!" I shouted, with my hand outstretched in protest. I didn't trust myself in that moment. I didn't recognize myself. I scared myself.

I stayed standing there with my hand outstretched; Corazón and I locked eyes from across the kitchen. A few moments passed, and then I slumped down on to one knee, my head hanging. Quickly, I, Emily, came into my body to the confused and scared eyes of my daughter. Next, thoughts of guilt, shame, and words of apologies washed through me and out my mouth. Still kneeling down, I offered her a hug. She approached me eagerly. Holding her small body against my chest, I was also holding and hugging myself. I wanted to scrape together a teachable moment from the hell I'd unleashed and said out of breath: "Mommy is doing a lot right now, and Mommy got really frustrated and overwhelmed. I'm so sorry I yelled so loudly. It scared you. It scared me, too. Know that no matter what comes out of my mouth, I always love you."

"No matter what, you always love me," she said as she hugged me tighter. We stayed there for some moments more. As we did, the frenetic current slowed throughout my body. After a breath, I heard crying and remembered my other child. With one last squeeze of Corazón's middle, I stood up, turned around, and walked down the picture-lined hallway to Juliet's room. The voice of shame chimed in, saying, *Wow! That was close! You almost hit your kid that time. What's gotten into you?*

Among the ocean-blue walls of Juliet's calming room, I scooped up her crying body and held her to my shoulder. I hugged her again, rocking her gently, muttered apologetically into her ear: "Lo siento, lo siento. De veras te amo. Perdóname!" Next, I thought: *I can't tell anyone other than Luke about this. What would they think of me? What if I had hit Corazón? Oh God!*

Back seated on the bench next to my mom, my gynecologist took my other hand and said, "You're a good mother asking for help." I wanted to believe her. I tried hard to. I felt like a failure. Next, she said she'd order some lab tests. I remember her saying that she wanted to check my prolactin levels. Then she stood and left the room to scrounge up a list of local psychiatrists; my mother hugged me, and I exhaled more fully. The bench was still intact.

Out of the waiting room and into the bright light of the summer day, my mother wanted me to call and make an appointment with one of the psychiatrists on the short list my doctor had just handed me. Walking to my car, I thought, *A psychiatrist?! A crazy person doctor, really? It's that bad. Now, I'm a crazy person?*

I sat in my car and dialed the first number. My mother sat in hers. One by one, down the list, I got the same answer: not taking new patients for two to three months. What? I called six offices. In an area with about 173,000 people, why was there not a single new patient psychiatric appointment after six calls?

With no success, I had to use the restroom before I parted ways with my mother. While I washed my hands, my eyes caught sight of a flier in the mirror. It was for a local postpartum depression support group. I dried my hands with a crisp brown paper towel and then turned and stepped closer. Not a single little flag with the organization's phone number was left, leaving the paper to appear shrunken. No new psychiatric appointments were available, and the support group flier had been stripped clean of information. These two truths equaled a struggling community in my estimate. I felt heaviness in my chest. Who was going to help me? What about my obstetrician?

Back home and still feeling embarrassed for ambushing my beloved gynecologist, I dialed my obstetrician's office. She had not been at the birth of Juliet, due to a family event, but we had a history. Back when I was pregnant with Corazón, Luke and I had started our prenatal care with a group of midwives. The first few appointments had gone great. Because it was a group practice, a different midwife attended us at each visit to ensure we met all the midwives by the time of delivery. At our appointment after our twenty-weeks anatomy scan, I think our practitioner was having a bad day because they didn't introduce themselves when they came in. They were also not very encouraging or enthusiastic. Honestly, they seemed apathetic. That worried me and was off-putting. It worried Luke, too. After discussing it between us, we decided we did not like having a revolving care provider. We wanted one. My mother's cousin was a midwife and professor. I happened to see her around then and got to ask her for advice. She encouraged me to listen to my desire for one care provider. She also said that she'd worked with some good obstetricians. Driving back from seeing her, I was hopeful we'd find a provider.

Since my prenatal appointments were still one month apart, I started asking around. I had a few acquaintances that were pregnant, too. I was also in a reiki training course with my friend and reiki master. One of my classmates seemed a good resource. She had a toddler, after having a stillbirth at full term, and had also adopted. Her mother was a midwife but retired. My friend had needed to transfer to the hospital to deliver her now toddler, and the obstetrician she had was a long-time colleague of her mother. It was the only obstetrician her mother could highly recommend because she'd saved my friend from having a cesarean section. If that wasn't an endorsement, I didn't know what was. Luckily, I was able to get into this obstetrician for a meet-and-see appointment. We met, and Luke and I shared our hopes of an unmedicated natural birth. It was comforting to learn, too, that our doula was one of her favorites. With that and more history between us now since Juliet's gestation, I was hopeful my obstetrician would help me in my hour of postpartum need.

The same afternoon as the gynecologist appointment, I left a message with the receptionist about why I was calling. I was asking for my obstetrician's psychiatrist recommendations. It wasn't thirty minutes later that she, personally, called me back. Gosh, it felt so good to hear her encouraging voice as I slowly paced around our balcony in the June sun. She said to call back and make an appointment to come in and see her the next day and that she could prescribe something if I needed it. After the disappointing psychiatrist office calls just a few hours earlier, that was supportive news. I smiled, and hope swelled in my chest. Luke shifted his work schedule around so we could see her together. I also looked into some mama support groups. There was one near her office, and with my appointment at 11 a.m. the next day, I thought I could go to the noon support group meeting, no problem. We had a plan.

By the time Luke and I met up and parked, in the familiar medical office parking lot of the obstetrician's office, it felt like a week had passed since I'd called, yet it was just the day before. I also felt really discouraged and ashamed it had come to this. Shame of needing help, professional help, pelted down on me like golf-ball-sized hail. My smile and optimism were long gone. Dread of judgment started to fill me. Sitting in the small waiting room, I saw pregnant bodies all around me; some faces looked tired, whereas others looked nervous. I was sure there was a scarlet letter F on my forehead for the others to see what a failure I was. When the nurse called us back, walking behind her down the hallways felt strange. Now the hallways felt constricting. It felt like she was taking me down the corridors of a cellblock to be punished. So ashamed of myself, I resigned myself to the reality that I needed professional help.

The appointment itself felt like I wasn't there. The Emily our doctor was used to seeing was not there; that was obvious. Sitting in the same chair I had sat in through Corazón's and Juliet's third-trimester checks,

I zoned out. I know the obstetrician talked to me, looked concerned, and then reassured me that I would "get through this." She named various medications whose names sounded familiar from television commercials. Luke sat a few feet away from me on a bench in the room, as there was no chair next to mine. At that short distance, he felt a world away. The obstetrician talked to Luke as the fellow professional that he was, and in that moment of intended collaboration, I felt as if they were ganging up on me. They both looked at me and talked to each other as if I wasn't able to hear them. The doctor saw how slowly I was talking and the flatness of my facial expression. Somehow my look was a diagnostic criterion that I was meeting for depression. Why did hearing that feel like a stab in the back versus reassurance? *God, I'm such a mess,* I thought to myself. I wanted to dissolve into thin air right then and there.

Next, there was talk about different medications and the various potential side effects, nausea being the most common. I said to my doctor and Luke: "I *hate* feeling nauseous. I'll certainly feel side effects. I'm scared to feel worse, particularly adding nausea to the mix, in an attempt to feel better. I don't know if medication is feasible." I felt sad and defeated, all the while feeling disoriented to the reality of the conversation.

"You have to take one to see," replied the doctor. I wasn't convinced. She wrote me a prescription and said she'd call me in a few days to check in. Luke and I walked back out to the lobby holding hands. I felt helpless and hopeless. He might as well have been leading me out, as I was leaning on him so much. I didn't feel like going to the support group. I just wanted to get home and lie down. Thoughts raced through my mind: *Wasn't the support group for new moms? Wasn't my postpartum time over at the three month mark? I'm a repeat mom, too, I'd really look a fool and Juliet is almost one. Won't it be moms with little babies? I don't want to be near a crying baby, right now.* I got into my car and drove straight home, avoiding the support group.

Luke had more time before his afternoon patients and met me at home. He'd have lunch and then go back to work. I didn't feel like eating. After walking in from the garage, I lay down on the sun-drenched couch. My skin warmed up as I curled into the fetal position. I felt nothing, frozen in place. I thought about nothing. I blankly stared out at our balcony windows at the sunny June day. Since we were home, our nanny, who'd been watching Juliet, left. Juliet was still napping down the hall. The longer I was on the couch, the more I doubted my ability to ever function as a human, let alone a mother. It was like I'd changed into a rock. Convinced of my eternal sedimentary transformation, I was surprised how it shattered at the first waking sounds of Juliet. As she fussed a little more, I took a deep breath, got up, and went to her. *I don't have time to feel depressed as a mother. I need to get some traction on feeling better, and fast,* I thought as I walked into her room and picked her up. I felt annoyed at life. Nagging feelings of guilt for not being a happy mother followed me around the house. I texted Luke, even though he'd just left, "Please get me some relief that won't give me side effects!" Then, Luke reassured me: "We'll figure this out. I love you." He said he'd text my acupuncture practitioner for ideas.

My practitioner, who treated me back in the fall of 2017, was transitioning out of Eugene at this point in June, due to life changes. However, before she left just weeks befor, earlier in the month, she put me in touch with a dual certified care provider in Portland. Dr. Y was both a naturopathic physician and practitioner of traditional Chinese medicine. I'd set up a new-patient appointment. It wouldn't be until mid-July, three weeks away. It seemed an eternity, but at least I had an appointment. I also made an appointment with a local naturopathic physician whose first opening for new patients was in October. Making the two-hour commute to Portland would be sustainable but only a few times.

I had not started taking any Chinese herb remedies, but I needed something. My practitioner reached out to Dr. Y knowing that I had the up-coming appointment. As if an answer to my unspoken prayers, Dr. Y replied with an amino-acid cocktail to help with my mood in the meantime until my appointment in July.

A few hours later, as Luke got dinner ready and the girls were playing, five white capsules rested in my hand as evening sunlight came through windows with a view. I'd been crying before Luke came home. The appointments of the last twenty-four hours didn't leave me feeling very optimistic. At this point, life felt curdled. Getting more rest, not working, and my counseling appointments seemed to mix poorly together and all I wanted was to feel good again. I wasn't convinced these supplements would help but why not. The alternative was the pharmaceutical prescription waiting for me at the pharmacy down the street.

The naturopath-acupuncturist assured us that amino acids would not hurt me. They worked like a selective serotonin reuptake inhibitor (SSRI)—effective and without the side effects. I swallowed the pills and sat down on our grey couch, the same one I rested on in a catatonic state at midday. I waited, hoping a miracle would happen. The static noise that roared in my head, paired with tingling agitation in my legs and arms, nagged at my soul. The time ticked by—five, ten, fifteen minutes. To distract myself, I watched white clouds slowly cruise across the blue June sky. After a bit, I sat and hung my head in defeat. Then it happened. I opened my eyes, slowly lifted my head, and looked out the window. The static was lessening; my body felt less agitated. It was like watching a drop of dish soap touch down into greasy water, scattering the grease towards the edges and leaving clearer water behind. My mind was clearing, and for a moment, I felt like me. I felt the most like "before"—before Juliet, before kids. Would it last? Was it possible to manage my mental health alternatively?

Chapter 8

The Body Remembers

My gut-knotting anxiety about taking pharmaceutical drugs for postpartum depression and anxiety was valid. When I was seventeen, I had a bad experience. The eleventh grade of high school was challenging for me. For as long as I could remember, I'd loved school, and school had been doable, even easy at times. My public high school, in the northeast part of Eugene, was known for its track and soccer teams. It also featured an international baccalaureate school, called the International High School, IHS for short. Ninth and tenth grades of IHS had been fun. My family's budgeted summer trips abroad, starting in fourth grade, with a five-week tour of Western Europe and a new destination summers running, complemented the global IHS curriculum I encountered. I had the real privilege of attending a private school program within my public school.

As a tenth grader, I fell in love for the first time. We'd been friends all of ninth grade. I babysat his little sister, and after his soccer practices we'd hang out. We dated for most of the tenth grade school year. My interests and focus were on my grades, my boyfriend, and my long-time friends, who were also focused on academics. My boyfriend's other friends were becoming more interested in parties, and he wanted to join them. My strong academic focus as well as my high standards for myself, my perfection, was holding him back. On the night of an awards ceremony, that celebrated my twelve years of participation and completion of an extracurricular club along with other members, he broke up with me with, saying, "I'm not in love with you anymore. Let's go back to being friends." Sitting next to him in the car, I believed him. I even thought, *That won't be hard; we were friends first.* As he drove away from dropping me back home, the reality started to hit me. I was crushed and utterly heartbroken. I cried inconsolably. The sadness I felt was worse than when my sister had lived abroad. I felt so alone. I sobbed on the floor of our carpeted hallway and curled up in a ball. My parents and visiting great-uncle and aunt comforted me into the night. The summer passed, and the new school year started. My heart had mended, and I was ready for a new year.

By eleventh grade, most classmates, myself included, had driver's licenses. With the freedom to drive, came the temptation to lie. In various social circles around me, I heard of weekend parties, which were synonymous with alcohol. These were events in which parents were not home or were not supervising. I wasn't ever invited to these parties. It didn't bother me or interest me. My classes were demanding for the first time. My five-year streak of almost perfect grades began to weigh on me.

I had to study hard to get the highest grades now. Dim, misty grey mornings, a few days a week, greeted me when I arrived early to school to get math tutoring. My global literature class, in a room with no windows and white painted cinderblock walls, was challenging, too. For that class, I read a whole extra book and completed an additional assignment to get an A. I had kept up the top grades, and my father continued to be proud to tears of me. When the report card arrived in the mail, I held my breath while I opened it, only to exhale with great relief that I'd met my goal again.

When my boyfriend broke up with me, he'd said he wanted to stay friends. At the time, I believed he'd meant it. However, that changed when we were in the same math class three months later. He'd gotten closer to his other friends after we broke up, and now they formed his inner circle. I was friendly when I saw him in class each day. I'd pass him and say, "Hey!" To that, there would be no response. The first couple of times it happened, I assumed he hadn't heard me. Then it became painfully obvious he had and was ignoring me. As the fall term approached the winter months, I started to feel really down about school and myself. My mother encouraged me to get regular exercise, and my parents bought me a gym membership thinking that physical movement would boost my mood.

With my license, I drove myself the ten minutes to the gym. It was nice to zone out watching television while I exercised on a cardio machine. Since about October, my body had started to feel different, like my skin was thicker than it used to be. My clothes started to fit funny, all over. Being supportive, my parents gifted me two months of fitness trainer sessions. With that coaching, I started logging my meals and ate regularly to keep up the muscle I was building. It worked! I was feeling better mentally, and my fitness was improving. But as January came around, the exercising didn't help my mood anymore. I also started to have regular bouts of constipation.

On a typical grey and rainy Oregon weekend in January, I started crying and stayed sad for days. That had never happened to me. I had had my childhood nickname of PD so moodiness was nothing new, but that sad mood was different. It wasn't PMS. It was something else. Later that week, I walked from my one-story green high school building to my pediatrician's office just down the street and around the corner. I went during the free-class period I had before my math class. Waiting for my appointment, seated on the violet-colored faux leather chair, I noticed the fish tank and its colorful fish as well as kid-sized toys in the foreground of my view. My pediatrician had been at my birth. He'd been in the operating room when I was lifted out of my mother. I told him about my recent crying and sad weekend and how hard school was. After talking for almost thirty minutes, he gave me a sample of Paxil, an antianxiety medication. Being seventeen, and trusting him completely, I took the sample pill there in the exam room. Then I retraced my steps to school and walked into my math class with a few minutes to spare before the bell.

While I sat and did my work, I started to feel off. I looked around at my peers. Did they feel the tightness in their chests, too? Everyone looked normal and was doing their work. I don't remember much after that, except that I started breathing hard and crying. My classmates started looking at me with big eyes, my ex-boyfriend included. I was so embarrassed. Would I be remembered as that girl who had a panic attack in fourth-period math?

When I got home, I told my parents what happened. My mother was furious with my pediatrician. She called his office before he'd left for the day. They talked for nearly an hour. She wanted to know why he'd prescribed a medication to me, a minor, without talking with her or my father. After what happened in math class, I didn't want to take pharmaceuticals. To me, I'd had a full-blown panic attack after taking an antianxiety medication. I'd felt out of control and like a stranger to myself. If that was what taking medication was like, I wanted nothing of it. The next thing I knew, my mother was on the internet, tapping the desk with a pencil as she waited for the dialup connection. She was looking up alternative treatments for anxiety and depression in teens. Looking over her shoulder, I watched as she purchased a light box, which was used for light therapy. From my mother's research, I seemed to have met criteria for seasonal affective disorder, or SAD. As I read another article she'd found, it said that SAD could start in adolescents. I passed the remaining monochromatic winter weeks eating breakfast in front of the full-spectrum light bulbs that blasted from a white rectangular box. My own personal sun sat on our kitchen table without the fear of ultraviolet rays. After two weeks, I felt happier more of the time. In those same weeks, I also started seeing a counselor about my stress. I remember their comfortable therapy room in an office downtown. I would go alone, and my parents joined in some sessions, too. After a month of light therapy and psychotherapy, I felt like myself again—at least my moods did. My digestion, however, was a whole other matter.

All winter that year, I had weeks of constipation followed by weeks of the opposite. I felt the worst when I was constipated. I had no appetite yet knew I needed to eat. During the months of therapy, my digestion improved. After leaving the pediatrician who had given me Paxil, I started seeing a nurse practitioner. She was overseeing my care now as my primary care provider. However, our relationship did not last long. The counselor I saw deemed my course of treatment, light therapy, sufficient enough to treat my stress and depression, and I was discharged. However, per the nurse practitioner, the return of my constipation and diarrhea was the result of stopping the counseling. The nurse tested my thyroid and other metabolic functions through blood tests. All of them came back within normal results. In her eyes, everything checked out okay. Since the labs were normal, she said, "Try some more counseling; that seemed to solve the problem before." She seemed to imply the problem was all in my head, and my symptoms were made up. But something felt off inside me, and I was angry with her. Why would I lie? I told my mother I didn't want to see her again for not believing me. Thankfully, my mother believed me. She believed my digestion issues and bodily sensations, like feeling that my skin was too tight, went beyond counseling. We did not return to that healthcare provider, and my mother went searching the internet for what was ailing me and for someone to help us.

The remaining months of eleventh grade were a blur. Being the second to last year of high school, the academic demands continued to increase in preparation for college applications. There were baccalaureate certificate exams I wanted to take so I could earn college credits before graduation as well as the Scholastic Aptitude Test, the infamous SAT. And wrapped around and through all these academic demands were my struggles with my physical and mental health. I worked arduously to get the grades and prepare for the exams; I so desperately believed I needed to do well to keep my sense of self. To prepare, I regularly did hours of homework. I studied past my parents' bedtime in my blue-walled room and at my wooden desk. My health symptoms continued to worsen to the point that my parents, who were also teachers, advocated for academic accommodations. With documentation, I was able to get a time accommodation while taking the SAT and could take as long as I needed to complete the exam. My symptoms of impaired cognition, including falling asleep in class, and poor digestion snowballed out of control as the last eight weeks of the school year stretched out before me.

I distinctly remember one overcast day in May. My parents had come to my school to attend a meeting with the school counselor. From their experience as teachers, my parents saw that my health issues, and the impact they were having on my declining mental health, qualified me for academic accommodations beyond the SAT. These supports consisted of pass/no-pass grading for my assignments for the remainder of the school year versus the typical letter grade scale. My hard earned A grades were intended to secure me academic scholarships in college. Since I'd kept impeccable grades throughout high school, I wanted to cash them out and save my parents money on my college tuition. Their advocacy worked, and I was granted the pass/no-pass accommodation for the remainder of the school year.

Driving home that day, I tried to comprehend the sanctuary they'd provided for me from the demands of school. I was free from the academic pressures. My hard work would be protected. I felt relaxed for the first time in a long time. I turned on the radio and Nelly Furtado's "I'm Like A Bird" was playing, a favorite of mine. It was as if the universe had seen my struggles.

However, with my symptoms worsening, my mother logged more hours scouring the internet. Her tireless devotion yielded an appointment, four states away, in Rochester, Minnesota, at the prestigious Mayo Clinic. It was my mother's home state, and we stayed with my grandmother in her brown condominium building. I missed the last two weeks of eleventh grade to attend the week of appointments. Across ten days, I collected my own urine for twenty-four hours in a milk-like jug, completed stress tests of my cortisol, in which I felt like I'd run a marathon, and used a wheelchair. There was the electro-current assessment, the intestinal endoscopy, and a psychological evaluation complete with the Rorschach test. They even gave me a pregnancy test for good measure. The diagnosis, after days of literal poking and prodding, was a somatoform disorder. In other words, stress was making me physically ill. The treatment: more counseling.

That was the summer of 2001, and my sister had been living in Japan since graduating from college in 1996. From afar, she'd been following my health issues via emails and phone calls with our mother. In August, my sister came home so the four of us could attend family therapy. We all met with the new counselor, the grandma-aged one, I'd started seeing at the end of May, just before traveling to Minnesota. Together, we reviewed our family history, particularly when I was little. After a handful of sessions that week, I had a major realization. With the help of the counselor, and more maturity at seventeen than as a five year old, I saw how I'd falsely understood my sister's language immersion experience in Japan when I was young. All those years, I believed my parents had sent her away. During our group sessions, it was also clarified that the few loud arguments between her and our mother had been typical teen-parent disagreements. Until then, I had surmised that because my sister argued with our mother, she had been sent away. These insights drastically changed how I saw my childhood and my teenage self. I would work with that same counselor through grade twelve and even into college to continue to review the revelations

I experienced that summer afternoon.

My twelfth-grade year was more enjoyable, with fewer physical symptoms, and I achieved my goal of sustaining my nearly perfect grades. The symptoms were less intense but still present—even after I graduated and completed a nine-month exchange to Argentina. In the picturesque Lake District of Patagonia, my moodiness dissipated, yet my unexplained weight gain, constipation, and missed periods persisted. Thanks to my devoted mother, upon returning from South America and through my undergraduate studies, I worked with various naturopathic physicians. Their diligence and commitment to me started to yield results when I was twenty-one. My health was greatly improved upon learning I had intestinal parasites and yeast as well as food sensitivities to gluten and diary. In February 2006, after a two-hour drive to Oregon City, I met the best and last doctor I'd work with. This doctor wanted to know my health history from my experience; he wanted a holistic ethnographic description, my description, instead of only relying on what my medical chart said. After hearing my story, he did a physical exam, and the results were indicative of a subclinical hypothyroid diagnosis. As 2006 went on, this doctor used complementary medicine; he prescribed Chinese herb formulas for digestion as well as pharmaceutical antifungal medication for systemic yeast. I felt respected and heard at each appointment, and my health greatly improved. With his guidance, I eradicated the imbalanced gut flora through strong antifungal pharmaceuticals. The rapport we developed over the course of my treatments dissipated any concerns I might have had about the potency of the medication he prescribed. As part of the protocol, for example, he frequently tested my liver enzyme levels and prescribed herbal supplements to offset any potential liver damage the drugs might cause. I ultimately learned how to manage my physical and mental health via my diet, supplements, and my annual light therapy. I would need to keep up these habits to keep my health intact.

Remembering those old fears I had about pharmaceutical interventions in my postpartum period with Juliet made me feel like I was time traveling. I was desperate to feel better, yet my fear of feeling more out of control by the possible side effects of antidepressants made them not a viable option. What would help me? Taking a deep breath, I thought back to when getting help for my health had resulted in improvement and wellness. Recalling the validation from the helpful doctor of my past felt like applying Aloe Vera to a sunburn. He'd used both alternative and allopathic Western methods to get me back to health, so I decided that I had to try and trust the new naturopathic physician and their amino acid combination. I also, however, became more curious about finding my own answers to questions about my mood.

Chapter 9

Knowledge Is Power

I was finally alone, thanks to the nanny. (The kids were overdue for the company of a happy and rested adult.) After driving to my in-laws' empty house, I sat, knees to chest, with a bulky blanket awkwardly draped around my slouched shoulders, and I exhaled. I soaked up the cozy noonday June sun on the longest day of the year. It was eight weeks since I drove away from my work parking lot, hope in my chest. Sitting there at my in-laws', I felt little and insignificant as well as lost and unknown to myself. Before I left the house, I didn't have the energy to engage with the girls, to be on. Taking refuge elsewhere, I mentally journeyed back in time. I daydreamed, as I gazed at a perfectly cloudless blue sky.

It was the longest day of the year, but still I felt as blasé, numb, lethargic, and depressed as the first winter I learned I had SAD at seventeen. How? "I. Am. Depressed," I repeated the words out loud into the expanse above me. I hugged my knees closer to my chest. "I'm depressed." As I looked up from my self-hug, I felt as far removed from my sense of self as my city, which appeared on the horizon. Even with a drowsy mind and drooping eyelids, I needed to pinpoint when my life got off track from how I thought I would be living with two kids. I couldn't be the only mother who felt numb, ambivalent, and dreaded parts of motherhood like I did, so I mentally reviewed the events of the last year to myself, starting with the present:

June 2018: I was professionally diagnosed with postpartum depression and anxiety and had lab work done after seeking help from my gynecologist. I started taking the amino-acid cocktail from the naturopath-acupuncturist after feeling like a failure in my OB's office and spent four days in group therapy.

May 2018: I started seeing a counselor and getting acupuncture weekly and began my leave of absence from work.

April 2018: I slept three hours a night because Juliet's arm was healing; we had our kitchen remodelled, and I did dishes in the bathtub.

March 2018: Eight-month-old Juliet broke her arm.

February 2018: Corazón had a fever for five days, and I had a sinus infection while I solo parented for a week.

January 2018 to November 2017: I had mini-breakdowns and meltdowns about every twelve days after going back to work at four-months postpartum.

October 2017: I was only able to nurse Juliet on one breast and supplemented her feeding with goat milk formula.

September to August 2017: I loved my sleep and feeding schedule with my two-month-old and felt happy with two kids.

July 2017: I finally delivered my second healthy baby vaginally after thirty minutes of pushing, which were preceded by seven hours of Pitocin. I had an epidural after seventeen hours of working naturally for labor to start after my water broke at home on our red couch.

Whoa! That had been a full twelve months, I thought to myself. *No wonder I'm so tired.*

The depressed headspace I was in was not where I imagined I would be weeks before Juliet's first birthday. What the hell happened? After recapping my postpartum months thus far, I felt chilled and wrapped the blanket tighter around me. In an attempt to rationalize, and think my way out of my personal nightmare of feeling depressed, I conducted a second review of my postpartum noticing major impressions:

- I had minimal sleep for over twenty days in a row, which never happened with Corazón.
- I did not breastfeed Juliet as long as I had Corazón, four versus ten months.
- I needed Pitocin for seven hours while delivering Juliet but only one hour with her sister.
- With Juliet, my water broke at home, and even after seventeen hours of trying natural forms of induction, there was no real start to labor.

- With Corazón, in contrast, my water was broken by my OB in the hospital after not breaking spontaneously and being eight centimeters dilated.

Okay so my second labor was very different from my first. I had Pitocin longer, but so what? Even though I was depressed, I now had a puzzle to solve: Did Pitocin play a role in how I currently felt? Could the receptors in my brain have become overloaded with synthetic oxytocin? If they were flooded, my body might have stopped or slowed down its natural production of oxytocin. Could that ultimately be why I'm depressed now? The scientist in me came alive with a question: Did my prolonged exposure to synthetic oxytocin put me at risk for depression at eight-months postpartum? That question gave me hope. I felt a slight lift in my mood with the chance that my depression could have a cause other than my own shortcomings. I cracked a smile, the first time in a long time. With my question in mind, I stood up and stretched my arms to the sky. My growing curiosity got me moving. I folded up the blanket and headed back home. I had research to do.

Later that afternoon, Luke and I looked together for answers in peer-reviewed medical journals. He searched PubMed looking for articles with terms like "pitocin and postpartum depression." We found an article that sounded like they had tested my question. The authors' hypotheses were that the synthetic oxytocin would reduce the risk of depression. However, their study showed that women who had prolonged exposure to Pitocin and who had a history of depression had an increased risk for postpartum depression. There was a connection between Pitocin and postpartum depression. "I was right, Luke!" I said, almost shouting and with tears welling in my eyes. A wave of relief washed over me. I needed to sit down to take it all in. *It wasn't my fault. It was not my fault. It was not my fault. It. Was. Not. My. Fault*, I chanted in my head, my body melting into our grey couch. If finding that article yielded some relief mentally, what else could I learn about postpartum brains that could help explain my behavior over the past five months?

With the nanny at home looking after the kids some afternoons, I took my laptop to a corner coffee shop just up the street from Luke's acupuncture office. Either before or after an acupuncture session, I would go there, order a latté, sometimes with cardamom and honey, and search peer-reviewed articles on postpartum depression. It became another form of therapy. Since learning about Pitocin, I got curious about how a mother's brain changed during pregnancy. After typing "postpartum brain changes" into the search bar of a journal database, I started reading the top hits. I read about how during pregnancy a woman's brain was "pruned" as drastically as during adolescence, and other areas of the brain were fortified.

Another article stood out to me on another day at the coffee shop. It was about sleep issues in mothers in the late postpartum period, or past three-months postpartum. I read about how babies were finding sleepy rhythms, but mothers were not. Home environments, noise, disorganization, and lack of routines were sources of stress in the study's participants and therefore possible causes of maternal sleep disruption independent of children. I sipped my latté and then remembered my own season of not sleeping.

Jetlag—that's the closest comparison to how sleep deprivation affected me. Starting at five-months postpartum with Juliet, I tried to push past the fatigue of the night, with its four wakeups, and go to work. I was being tortured by a love of my life. Coffee caffeine became my drug of choice. It got me to lunchtime, and then with a hope and a prayer I'd make it through to bedtime. By the eight-month mark postpartum with two kids, I saw firsthand the intimate relationship between sleep and mental function.

And it wasn't just Juliet who was keeping me awake at night and preventing a restful sleep. There were also the neighborhood goings-on that played on repeat, always in the wee hours of the night. There were the pop pop pop sounds I heard one night that had me roll over and try to make out the sounds. Trying to listen I heard music noises, then slap...slap, the sound of something landing on the ground. Next, I sat up and glanced at the red numbers on the clock across the room on Luke's side table: 1:14 a.m. Then, I heard three car doors slam shut, one, then two right after each other. *What just happened?* I thought to myself as I heard a car speed off. Bleary-eyed and headachy, from already waking up twice with Juliet, I collapsed into my sheets and prayed for sleep to envelope me.

The sequence of that night continued to play out every night, like clockwork for months. The second night it happened, I got out of bed. I was pissed and spied out the window. Our house sits on a hill, at the corner of a T in the road. The juncture made a natural amphitheater, and I added a visual to the sounds I'd heard the night before. I heard it: Pop. Pop. Pop. And three car doors opened. Two people then got out, and the passenger opened a rear door to let a dog out. The driver walked and threw newspapers on my neighbors' driveways. The radio was on in the car, and that night, it played talk radio. The fatigue in my bones flared, as I witnessed another night's disturbance that was out of my control.

Along with Juliet's sleep regressions, she also experienced teething, which was brutal, albeit short lived, as well as restlessness with her broken arm. As a result, there were nights I was up every forty-five minutes, the whole night. As soon as my body calmed enough to drift into sleep, she'd start crying again. We would give her a minute or two to try and resettle herself, but some nights, it took one of us to rock her back to sleep. It seemed like when she woke that often, *I* was the one awakened by it, not Luke.

As time went on, I began to dread going to bed. I knew that it didn't matter how well a night Juliet would have. Those darned newspapers were still going to be delivered. It happened right on time every night. Those weeks of little sleep were wrapped in and around my work schedule and a kitchen remodel. Headaches and brain fog became regular. As I drove from appointment to appointment for my job, my eyelids got heavier and heavier. I opened my car window to try and keep myself awake with the cool spring air. On one afternoon, someone honked at me because the light changed, and I didn't see it. I'd closed my eyes just for a moment. It was not good or safe. I felt myself fraying like an old rope, and I was getting down to the final fibers. So one day, I did something about it.

Listening carefully, I did my best to navigate the phone prompts that the newspaper press had on their automated answering service. At last, I was speaking to the circulation manager. The manager was a woman, and I was hopeful. I explained that I was not a customer, but that my neighbors were. I also shared how sleep deprived I was with my baby. As I heard myself speak, I compassionately saw my case and was proud of myself for speaking up and sharing my feelings.

"Might these deliveries be made closer to early morning hours versus in the middle of the night? I know my neighbors are not awake that early to read the paper," I said.

"That's very reasonable. I'll reach out to the route supervisor," the manager said. She then thanked me for calling.

As I pressed the red button on my cell phone to hang up, I sighed hopefully. I was realistic and didn't have high hopes that a change would happen immediately, although going to sleep that night, I did feel optimistic it would be different, even just a little.

The grind of life that month wore on. At times, I willed my eyes to stay open while sitting in front of my clients and their caregiving adult. I was exhausted. The nightly newspaper wakeups were still happening, though now at 4:30 a.m. I wasn't sure the three-hour time shift was an improvement, but at least it was different. The noises—three doors opening and closing and the sound of a car speeding down the street—continued. I couldn't be the only person on our street being disturbed, or could I? I needed to call the manager again. Did I dare? I needed to at least try. The worst that could happen was no change.

I pressed the corresponding numbers on the automated phone service again to reach the circulation manager. She remembered me and was glad to know things were better. Against all the cultural training I had not to complain as a woman, I shared my displeasure with the continued noise of the delivery team. I could hear my inner self-talk start to have an opinion: *You're asking a lot...* But was I? As I spoke, it took all my might to speak past my body wanting to shush the tension writhing around my torso and abdomen. I didn't want to annoy the woman. Society had groomed me, and plenty of other women, to try only to accept the slightest of improvements. But not this time. I was getting desperate to sleep. It had been a full month and Juliet's arm had healed perfectly, however, my sleep debt was now extensive. Something had to give.

The manager was glad to get an update from me that the delivery team had adjusted the time of their ruckus. However, she was not pleased to hear me report they were still speeding away down our street. She apologized for the continued disturbance. The tone in her voice told me she was determined to fix it, herself. She said she would personally reassign the rout that day. I was speechless yet could still utter my deepest gratitude. I hung up in awe.

I'd found an ally. The profundity of the support she afforded me flooded my whole being with relief. She had listened to me. When I woke the next morning at 6:30 a.m. by my own timing, tears welled in my eyes. No car doors opened or closed; no slapping newspapers landed on driveways, and no cars sped away. Somehow, I had slept through it all. I guessed I was that tired. More mornings went on like that, though. After a week, it was clear she'd come through, just like she said she would. My body relaxed. My sleep cycle reset. I was so thankful. I had been taken seriously. My self-advocacy worked.

Recalling the newspaper noisemakers and the late postpartum sleep article, I saw their connection and thought, *I knew there was a correlation between my stress levels and my restless sleep that put me over the edge when my eyes fell upon the piles of stuff all over the house!* Zooming out on my life to get more context was doing me a lot of good. Over time, I felt less neurotic, less crazy, and less like I was part of the problem. I had one more week left of my leave from my job, before returning for the five-week summer session. Curiosity and excitement began to creep within my body, along my legs and up to my chest in the form of effervescent tingles, and I plotted my next topic to investigate: my Latina heritage and identity. I reasoned that since my dad's five sisters all have at least two kids and appear happy, why couldn't I? As a Latina, wouldn't being a mom come naturally?

Chapter 10

Latina Enough?

Sitting near the corner window in my regular coffee shop, on my last Tuesday before my leave was up, I wondered whether much research existed on Latina mothers and postpartum depression. Since I am half Mexican, I was curious whether my ethnicity played a part in how I was feeling. While I searched for articles on links between being a Latina and postpartum depression, I reflected on how I came to identify as a Latina.

In the mid-to-late 1980s, there were not many middle-class Mexican Americans in Eugene, Oregon. There was no context, in my predominantly white world, for Spanish-speaking middle-class families because there were none, other than my own, that I knew of. My father was acculturated to mainstream US culture and believed that speaking Spanish to me would slow, impair or confuse me and my English learning, so he didn't teach me Spanish. I heard him speak Spanish every Sunday, however, when he called my grandparents' house in the agricultural town of Nyssa, Oregon, eight hours east of Eugene, and sitting on the Oregon-Idaho boarder. I pronounced my last name with the correct, interdental "th" sound for the "d" with pride. For a long time, that was one of the few things I could correctly say in Spanish. Other than my last name, one would never know that I was half Mexican. When thinking of names for me, my parents considered how others might struggle to say an ethnic first and last name, so they chose a first name that was easy to say; it turned out to be one of the most popular girl names of 1983.

My light skin had strangers asking if my father was someone other than the dark-skinned man holding me on his shoulders. Days after I was born, my father's college friend called to congratulate my parents and also asked, "What does she look like?" A question that really meant "How dark is she?" My father's family made comments about skin color too, a reflection of their colorism. I was the daughter of azul, or blue, as his family teased my father for the darkness of his skin. Over the years, I hated hearing strangers say, with false authority, "You don't look half Mexican." Compared to my father and his siblings, and most of my cousins, I didn't have darker skin and black hair like them, so for a long time, I didn't see or identify myself as Latina.

Although my name and my skin did not give away my partial heritage, there were invisible things that set me apart from other kids because I was Latina. It showed up when I would visit a friend's house for a meal and they would cook Mexican food. I realized that not all kitchens had a large, round, cast-iron griddle, or comal, to warm up store-bought tortillas on. Nor did they know how to keep them warm—that is, wrapped in a clean kitchen towel and then placed in a basket or bowl. I looked confused when I saw cold tortillas being put in the microwave or not heated at all. Looking my best outside the house was also important. I don't remember complaining much about being dressed up by my mother, bows in my hair and everything. My father instilled in me the value of keeping my clothes pristine. He knew personally that the world did judge books by their cover, and I as an extension of him was going to get a good rating. I also felt a need to make my family proud by my behavior. To reinforce that, consciously or not, I knew the story about my father's twin sister, who was kicked out of the family home at sixteen.

My Tía came home past curfew because her boyfriend's car had broken down. Her twin, my father, was to be her chaperone, but the two made a meet-up plan after they left the house together. When she didn't show at the meet-up location, he eventually went home without her. My grandmother assumed the worse. She assumed that my Tía was damaged goods, and unless she moved into her boyfriend's home and married him, the community would shun our family, according to my grandmother. Although that might have been true, my grand-mother's reputation in the tight-knit migrant farm worker community seemed to be more important than believing my Tía that nothing happened (sexually) and welcoming her home. Sadly, my grandfather could not convince my grandmother otherwise. The impact of that assumption rippled down through the family and my Tía's life.

Ironically, there was a Spanish-immersion elementary school program two miles from my childhood house. It was attended by primarily, if not solely, white kids. My parents tried for three years to enroll me, but I never won the lottery entrance process. Much older cousins from Texas had come and danced at that school one year in their broad ribboned skirts that they held up with straight arms or on to their hips. As they twirled and danced, with their dark hair braided and piled on the sides of their heads with colorful ribbons, I so wanted to attend the school, I so wanted to be counted as authentic like them. After not getting in by second grade, my parents gave up. Not getting into the bilingual school, however, sparked a desire in me. I was determined to one day become bilingual. My journey to learn Spanish somewhat fluently had me take classes with friends in middle and high school and cross paths with many memorable teachers. Strong friendships were forged, and countries were visited. Gradually, from the age of twelve, I constructed a bilingual self another way. It was while on an exchange for nine months to Argentina that being Latina began to feel authentic.
    As a gap year between high school and starting college, I went to live in the northern Lake District of Patagonia, in the province of Neuquén, Argentina. During my nine-month stay in Argentina, I traveled all over the country. In my last few months there, I was mistaken for a local when I was with friends in Buenos Aires. Argentina was a country with many European descendants, many of whom had fairer complexions than I did. Seeing other European-looking people speaking Spanish helped me to accept myself, my Latina self. It offered a new possibility to myself as a lighter-colored Latina who had never seemed dark enough, Latina enough.
    While still on exchange, my parents came to visit. With help from new friends and their families, I arranged for us to stay in downtown Buenos Aires for a few days after collecting my parents at the airport. My hair was longer and wavy, something different than my before Argentina self. Large dangly earrings hung from my lobes in place of shorter ones or studs from my earlier teen years. I was blooming into myself, a Latin self.

On their first night there, my father and I walked together down the block from our modest hotel and around a corner to a telefónica, a telephone shop. The bright florescent lights of the place, with its clear-partitioned booths, one after another, around the three sides of the shop, made us squint. After stating we'd be making an international call to the US, we were assigned a booth along the right-side wall. Sitting on my father's lap to fit, I dialed the number that my father had unfolded from a scrap of paper he'd tucked into his black leather wallet behind a toddler picture of me and a posed portrait of his parents in plastic photo sleeves. My grandfather answered the phone. With the time difference, it was afternoon in Nyssa. My Abuelo and I chatted about my parents' arrival, and he teased me about my new Argentine accent. *Better a Spanish with an accent than no Spanish at all,* I thought.

That was my first phone call to them, but my grandmother had sent me a few letters while I was on my exchange, a huge accomplishment with her eighth-grade education. Her writing skills were just perfect for my reading abilities in Spanish. The topic of weather used to be all that I could talk about with my grandparents besides some niceties I'd learned in Spanish class. As I chatted away with fluency, I looked at my father over my shoulder and shifted off his lap and wedged myself next to him. His eyes were wet, and he smiled as he wiped them. I transitioned the conversation to include passing the phone to him where he took the receiver and shared a greeting before we said goodbye. Hanging up, he turned to me and said, still wiping his eyes and shaking his head in disbelief: "You did it. You're bilingual." Having somewhat mastered a previously mysterious language, granted me access to a new identity and later to more knowledge about my heritage.

Back home in college, my journey to fortify my newly gained language proficiency continued. I worked on my writing in Spanish and reading among other hispanohablantes, or Spanish speakers, who like my father grew up speaking Spanish but had no education to read or write it. The mix of individuals was as colorful as the places where Spanish is spoken. My inability to communicate with my grandparents for the majority of my childhood gave me insight into individuals who lose their ability to communicate when they have a stroke. That connection pointed me in the direction of my profession as a speech-language pathologist and therapist. Once I knew what profession would suit me, my focus has always been to serve Spanish-speaking families.

I saw it as a way to keep up my Spanish that I worked so hard to learn and, most importantly, to give back to the Spanish-speakers in Eugene who were a growing yet marginalized community—a similar type of community my father had been a part of as a child. With my newly gained language skills, determination, and professional degrees, I savored a new identity, too: Latina.

For six years, before getting pregnant with Corazón, I conducted home visits to the crowded apartment complexes with one-way driveways or to the large trailer parks on the edges of town. Seated on the family couch, I saw many Spanish-speaking mothers happy and capable of mothering. These mothers took care of their children, and their neighbor's kid too sometimes, for extra income, all day long, in the small space of an apartment or trailer. They also kept the house clean, and cooked. It never occurred to me that they might not have loved every moment of their lives or had even raised their voice in frustration when I wasn't there. And in my position of providing individualized and assessable communication education as a speech-language pathologist, I represented the system. They were under my surveillance concerning not only their child's progress but also their mothering. It's not surprising that they kept it together during my one-hour visits. Not realizing the full extent of the influence of my presence on their behavior, or really the hegemonic system I was personifying, I created the narrative, for all these years, that the Latina mothers I worked with loved all of motherhood all of the time. *One day, I would, too,* I thought. When I met Luke in my mid-twenties, I was not certain I wanted to have children, nor was he. However, as thirty started to appear on my horizon, a longing ignited in my core.

The year before we successfully conceived Corazón, and while I was pregnant, I had read little about pregnancy and parenting because I didn't think I needed to. I believed, with all my being, that because I had a uterus and felt feminine that I would automatically be motherly and nurturing. In my head, I thought of my father's mother, my Abuela. She appeared to know how to mother having had thirteen kids, including two sets of twins. With half of my blood and genetics from Mexico, I was confident in my mother self. I staunchly believed I had done motherhood for lifetimes. I whole-heartedly believed that I could and would intuit my pregnancy, postpartum, and motherhood. I was female so therefore I would know. Maternity was my birthright, or so I thought.

My Abuela held a strong belief that motherhood and wifedom were wonderful and the epitomes of a woman's existence. There was no space for an alternative or less than marvelous experience, and I never questioned that. In good magical-realism fashion, I imagined my grandmother watching me (she died on Corazón's due date) while I struggled to enjoy the blessing of being a mother. I felt ashamed. In those months of feeling overwhelmed and irritated, I felt as if I were disappointing my heritage. Was I the only Latina wondering if motherhood would ever be more enjoyable?

When I felt overstimulated by Juliet's crying and Corazón's precocious questions, especially on the stretch of days when Luke was out of town, I would remember all those families, all those Latina mothers. There were many of them, over the years, who were at a glance getting along, and there I was having a hard and miserable time. I felt I had no right to complain. The notion of complaining in my Mexican family was not socially acceptable. I wanted to be a good daughter and a good granddaughter, and so I kept silent and suffered.

Those days of perceived failure led to self-loathing. I thought of my father's sisters, who had birthed two to four kids each, and they seemed to be totally fine with the whole concept of motherhood. During once-a-year visits as a kid, to Eastern Oregon, I remember the low ceiling entryway and the wall of a thousand eyes that greeted visitors at the childhood home of my father. All four walls were plastered with posed family pictures of my thirty-five first cousins and their parents from the 1980s and 1990s. There were so many frames that I couldn't see the color of the walls. During those visits, I would watch my father smile, laugh, and speak in Spanish around the small black kitchen table with high-back black faux-leather chairs beneath a bare light bulb. On those visits, I felt like a foreigner in my own family. It was as if by magic to me that my cousins could understand Spanish from their parents and could understand our grandparents without an interpreter, unlike me. Their direct access to our grandparents was a secret source of jealousy to me. It lingers even now. In those short visits, my aunts were models of well-adjusted mothers, or so I assumed. They seemed happy and showed me that I came from a culture where mothers were happy in motherhood, yet as a repeat mother, I felt unhappy more than I had ever expected.

Mothering two daughters broadened my view of my mixed-ethnicity self. My ethnicity was like a braid of hair, some strands darker and others lighter. I began to see the weave of different ideas about mothering from my two different halves. I'd unknowingly worked on that braid my whole life. My observations from our visits to Eastern Oregon, in the small red house on the east side of the railroad tracks, provided context that I believed I needed to draw from as a mother. The media I watched and books I read also shaped my understanding of motherhood.

I recall my mother being happy most all of the time when I was a child, and that increased the internalized pressures when I wasn't, which was another source of guilt for me. My mother was the oldest of two brothers, and for various reasons, mostly geographical, I didn't visit that side of the family aunts as often. One aunt was white and worked full time; the other was Japanese and also worked. Both were primarily responsible for their children. From what I saw, the few times I did visit, they were happy, yet the honest realities of the private life are kept secret. How would I ever have known, as a kid or a teen, the complexities of adult inner worlds, let alone about anyone's mental health?

On my laptop at the coffee shop, I read through titles on the maternal mental health of Latina mothers. My eyes widened, in surprise, reading that Latinas had higher risk rates of postpartum depression. *That means me*, I thought. My gaze was glued to the black letters forming these words on the page. Moving my eyes carefully, from left to right, I read what could have been my own words when the participants shared their experiences. I breathed deeply, and my shoulders relaxed. I wasn't the only one. These women used the same language as my own. Their words conveyed the knotted and contracted internal struggle of what it is to ask for help and the weight of actual, or perceived, social shame if they confessed that motherhood was hard. Like me, they felt they'd be viewed as complaining or weak, as each knew someone who lived in much harder circumstances and was doing just fine, which just silenced them more. Suffering was synonymous with motherhood. Sitting back in my chair, I could feel my brain busily making new neural networks, and more of my postpartum struggles made sense. My body relaxed. I felt validated by what I'd read. I took a sip of my warm drink and read on.

With each line of the research I read, I felt more and more tension release from my body. It was as if I were holding up a mirror to myself and could see unexamined corners of my own shadow that I didn't know existed. The paragraph-long descriptions of traditional female roles stopped my reading. The word "traditional" clanged around in my head. As I kept reading, the word gripped my torso like a corset. I held my breath in astonishment. These descriptions of traditional female maternal roles might as well have had my face as the visual example. I was at once confused and ashamed. I believed I was a feminist and progressive. I had also been aiming to sustain super-mom agility— giving it my all both at home and at work. I gave so much effort amidst so many expectations. Yet I believed I was failing as a mother.

I read on and learned that women who put others' needs before their own in the name of dutiful motherhood experienced guilt and poor mental health. By trying to maintain an A+ in motherhood now as a mother of two—plus my high-achieving background as well as the cultural belief that had me believing that asking for help was a weakness—left me weary, irritable, and thinking I was a shit mom.

I looked away from my laptop screen; the reflection back to me was too much. Now my drink was gone, and my head was swimming. It was a mix of a buzz and a headache. Was it all those pieces of myself I'd remembered in those few hours of reflecting, researching, and reading? Was it the caffeine? I was days away from returning to my job, and now I had more questions and less time to answer them.

Chapter 11

Putting It into Practice

Turning off the car, I paused, hands resting at the base of my steering wheel, and took a deep breath. My leave-of-absence was over, and I was back at work. The five-week summer session serving children and their families had started and it would be my last. It was bittersweet. The new supervisor job was moving towards a firm contract. All areas of my life were ready for a change.

Feeling nervous and excited, I opened my car door and stepped out. Two short months earlier, I had stood in that same parking lot and set my initial professional boundary with my supervisor. That "no" ignited a chain reaction of reassessing and reevaluating many parts of myself. Did other mothers experience an internal remodeling of their mothering? I had burned the proverbial house down with my irritability and rage, which left what I was really made of steaming. I was a postpartum phoenix now. I gathered my workbag and hesitated. It was as if a twenty-something version of myself wanted to give up on this, my first day back, but another part of me wanted to show up. I'd been raised to finish what you start. I wanted to finish my nine-year tenure in a way that was in alignment with my true self—with integrity. I was different now. I had been broken apart in my breakdown, and I had not put back the pieces the same way as before. It was a breakdown to break through.

Returning to the familiar building and reconnecting with the same group of people showed me just how much work I had done on myself during my leave. I noticed my sensitivity to other people's energy. I noticed myself moving more slowly. My negative self-talk changed its tone of voice and gave me a running commentary: *Look, see, it's easy doing what you know. You don't need to think about changing jobs. Why would you gamble with something new when you know everything here? I mean nine years is a long time. You would be turning your back on a lot.*

As I talked with other colleagues, I sensed something new, like acquiring a new sense of emotional capacity. I was able to perceive the exact moments I felt deep sadness, a contraction in my chest, when colleagues shared challenging stories of the clients they were serving. Being more aware and knowing about so much pain and suffering as well as disappointment and loss, I realized it was something I needed to take a break from, at least for the time being. My nervous system couldn't cope.

After picking up my printing from the copier, I visited a friend and colleague in her office. I thought our interaction would be brief in her peaceful office, sea green walls with plants and an essential oil diffuser going, but she began to recall her own experience of postpartum anxiety. She surprised herself with her ability to remember. As she proceeded with details, I pulled up a chair.

My friend had been in a stressful job and had a nine-month-old. She had finished nursing and started a nutritional cleanse. Then, she described a full-blown panic attack that involved being wheel chaired to her school nurse's office, having a coworker drive her home and spending an extended weekend trying to understand what had happened to her. At the time, the only variable that could explain what happened was her new low-dose hormone intrauterine device (IUD). So she got it removed. It helped some, but she was still anxious. The fact she was nine months postpartum didn't occur to them or her doctors as relevant. She went on and looked off to the side, the way one does when recalling a vivid memory and it's playing out in their mind's eye.

Checking in with my body, I noticed I had been holding my breath, as I hung on to her every word. She had checked in on me as her busy life allowed during my leave from work. The remembering of what happened to her not once, but again with her second child during the same late postpartum time, confirmed why she'd listened so well to me. I'd felt she understood me more than she was saying. After finishing her story of a hard time in her life, she had a look of awe in her face. She went on to ask a rhetorical question, with a sigh of disbelief: "How could I have moved so far past all of that to have almost forgotten about it?" That was the first time she'd recalled or shared that story ever.

To ease the challenge on my system of returning to work for the summer session, Luke and I arranged for a few nights alone away at the Oregon coast. We left the kids with my parents. Driving the curvy roads through a mountain range, I felt free. Once at the ocean, we turned north and continued driving. The sky was cloudless. White waves sparkled against the green ocean and blue sky. By the time we arrived at our lodgings, I felt like a new person. I felt like myself—happy and optimistic.

Just five miles before reaching the spunky coastal town we liked to stay in, I dropped Luke off to enjoy a trail run. After checking in, I walked along the shoreline and found a bench to sit on. I sat there and enjoyed the sights and sounds around me.

Since being a child, I have always known about sneaker waves. These unpredictable waves take lives every year along the Oregon coast. One must never turn their back to the water. As I sat and marveled at the sheer force of the ocean, I felt a steadiness. I'd made it out. All those weeks since my reiki session and I hadn't drowned. I would live to see another tide of myself. As waves broke against the ageless rocks, the water leapt and slapped the hard surface of the shore. The waves' spray moistened the surrounding rocks. The presence of dense green algae suggested a long-standing rhythm—a long-standing relationship. Constant collisions were normal, expected, and healthy. White foam frothed on the surface and catapulted itself into the air. At its zenith, droplets hovered in midair, like an offering to the expansive heavens, suspended for a moment. Those waves, that day, took my breath away.

That unique moment would repeat until the sun dies, yet never again in that exact way. *I am this ocean. I, too, have tides*, I thought. Seasons of intensity passed through me. My mental and emotional states, and my body, were like ocean currents journeying across the globe submerged deep underwater. There, beneath the undulating surface before me, currents resembled umbilical cords. Those cords seemed to reach back to the past, to mothers and sisters linked by blood or circumstance. Those life and love lines anchored me, and all women, in the port of womanhood. In that turbulent season of my life, I would keep fighting to hold on to them.

I sat on the smooth wooden bench and waited for Luke while also enjoying some solitude. I was inspired to write and capture how the water moved me and seemed to show me who I was, who I'd been, and who I would become. Water is symbolic and sacred in many traditions. At that juncture in my life, since seeing and living through hurricanes of feeling overwhelmed, I felt called to take up the chalice of my body and honor my water, my red tide, my blood. It was when I bled that I needed the most rest.

Knowing that a tide doesn't change direction in a moment, I vowed to methodically establish steadfast self-love, self-compassion, and self-care, particularly during those times of large crashing waves. The ecosystems of a woman's bleeding depend on it. All her relationships depend on it. The ocean feels no shame surging, lapping, or devouring a coastline. Why should I? The ocean's never taken a day off, yet I'd learned it was paramount that I do. Resourcing myself was essential. Rest came in a natural rhythm. There was an ebb and flow. Being committed to my needs meant surrendering a form of perfection to instead be embraced and nurtured. With this commitment to myself, I would also risk disappointing people. I loved myself just enough now to be worth that risk. As if a baptism, the cool ocean mist refreshed my desire to get in sync with the phase-by-phase steps of my cycle. The ocean seemed to know herself magnificently, and I wanted that, too. I would learn how to rest and when to take the most action.

Inspired by the muse of the waves, I met back up with Luke for dinner. We went out to eat seafood. As our server asked our drink order, I felt an urge to order the sweet treat of a Shirley Temple. Instead of suppressing the urge, I indulged my inner child and ordered the colorful drink. It made me smile. It was healing to yield to my frivolous needs because I could. The break from mothering and the routine of caregiving was restorative. The weekend was a welcome opportunity to appreciate the hard work I'd been doing on myself. I would never stop fighting for what I loved, especially myself.

One evening, a few days shy of returning to work, and after a particularly irritable day, I recalled faintly the title of a book shared with me by a caring acquaintance some months before on social media. I hunted for her message and the title. Reading the message thread, in the evening light, I found the title and bought the book with one click.

Molly Caro May's book, *Body Full of Stars: Female Rage and My Passage into Motherhood*, became an anchor. I started reading it slowly. Images of her own struggle were at times too similar to my own to keep reading. But seeing the book lying on my night-side table comforted me. "If she'd felt rage and lived to tell about it, so could I," I told myself.

Two weeks after I first held the hard-covered, cream-colored book, Caro May announced an upcoming workshop with author Kimberly Johnson of *The Fourth Trimester* in Montana. Without hesitation, I signed up that day. I'd never been to Montana before. I wondered how fall would look at that latitude. I booked my Airbnb and bought my plane ticket. As I hit the final click, I knew in the deepest parts of my soul that I had made a date with destiny and a healthier future self. The prospective trip kept me going to counseling and to the upcoming appointment with Dr. Y, the naturopathic and Chinese medicine doctor. My new supervising job waited for me, too, sparkling on the near horizon, as I worked through my final week of my job. I would keep going, remembering the phoenix that I was. Although I had the new job on the horizon, there were a few instances throughout my leave when I plumbed the depths of myself, and for a few seconds, dark inklings of suicide appeared fuzzy in my mind. My fear of missing out on life saved me from translating those inklings into clear thoughts of taking my own life.

Just days after my tall slim colleague and office mate of nine years helped me put the last box of preschool therapy activities in my car, I drove north to Portland for my appointment with Dr. Y. My brain and thoughts felt light and airy driving the two-hour journey as I whizzed past farmland, over rivers, and through towns. I reflected thoughtfully on my final home visits with families and savored the final session one-on-one with Spanish-speaking preschoolers. Their smiles, innocent humor, and friendship would be missed.

Listening to my phone navigation carefully, I made turns onto one-way streets and then found the address for the appointment in a former library. A wall with graffiti adjacent to where I parked across the street, at a two-hour parking sign, seemed to mock the regal pillared entrance to the former city building. I was a few minutes early and found the restroom after winding through the hallway. Just before the restroom door on the right, there was the entrance to a meditation hall on the left. Using the toilet and washing my hands, I took in the details of the old restroom—the white subway tiles on the walls and high ceilings. Walking out, I stopped and read the bulletin board belonging to the meditation community. It was comforting and logical that the physician's practice was neighbors with a meditation group. Healing happens inside and out.

It was a Saturday, and there was no receptionist working. After walking through the door, a pleasant chiming of some bells announced my entrance. I took a seat and waited for the doctor. I was hopeful that she could help me. It had been two whole months since I'd learned about Dr. Y from my own acupuncturist and had been helped by the amino-acid combo that afternoon in June. They'd become part of my daily routine and were stabilizing. While waiting, I was reminded of the moment my mother and I'd arrived at the office of another physician in Oregon City in 2006. Just as then, a nervous sense of uneasy hope fluttered in my stomach. Working with that doctor proved to turn the health issues of my teen years all the way around and yielded a level of wellness and health that rendered me unrecognizable to him when I sent him a copy of my wedding announcement four years later. It was with a sense of curiosity and faith that I stood up and walked into Dr. Y's office.

She directed me to a comfortable overstuffed chair that sat opposite her big wooden desk. Her tall height surprised me. Knowing from past experience that initial appointments with naturopathic doctors were lengthy, I settled in. After waiting so long for this appointment, I was going to enjoy every second. We started talking, and in the course of thirty to forty-five minutes, I summarized my turbulent health history and my postpartum crash. Her questions incorporated her dual training, and being the wife of an acupuncturist, I appreciated how they complemented the two healing styles and ideologies. It was clear from the beginning that our working relationship together would be short lived, as I lived two hours away, but she gave my intake just as much focus as if we would work together for years.

Dr. Y could see overarching patterns in the types of issues I had as a teen and my current symptoms of adrenal depletion and fatigue in my postpartum period. She informed me that my symptom of bone-tired fatigue, for example, was due to my adrenal glands not keeping up with hormone production. Over time, and due to chronic stress, that supply chain caught up with my body. Like a good naturopathic physician, she educated me on the various supplements she was going to put me on, including one made from the adrenal glands of cows, pigs, and sheep to get my body back up and functioning. Talking with her and hearing her give me clear explanations for why I felt exhausted, irritable, and miserable let me fully exhale. During the physical exam and while taking my blood pressure, she described to me the energetic theme that she suspected was beneath all of my past and current health issues: I had poor boundaries. She did not just mean my struggle to have boundaries with Corazón or my history of gut issues with permeable intestines. I also had to create boundaries with my mother or people I didn't want to disappoint.

As Dr. Y peeled back the noisy Velcro of the blood-pressure cuff, I remembered lying in the wide hospital bed wearing little more than an oversized cotton gown. I was twenty-six hours into labor with Corazón. My mother excitedly hovered outside my door and frequently requested to come in and see me. Her initial attempts had been met by my message, relayed by Luke, of not now. In that moment, I believed she would not acknowledge a boundary I had established. My inability to ever say "no" to her had been the status quo of our relationship for as long as I could remember. Until then, conscious or not, my parents' emotional wellbeing was my prominent priority. It trumped my own needs and stunted my ability to identify them.

Back on the freeway, not two hours later, I held the steering wheel with relaxed and steady hands. Small glass bottles of animal glands lay in the passenger seat next to me, and I'd taken a dose before leaving the office. My next appointment was in a few weeks in September. Taking a deep breath, I sighed out long and felt a huge sense of relief loosen the muscles of my neck and shoulders, as I knew I would have more energy and would not feel like shit for forever. Surprisingly, Dr. Y and I shared birth dates. That made me smile. Dr. Y impressed upon me the impact of the physical depletion that comes from pregnancy and postpartum. Looking across the agricultural landscape that skirted the freeway, I thought to myself, *I'm not weak or a failure. I'm depleted and need time to replenish all areas of my life and it's going to take awhile.* Driving home, I felt saved from the fear of feeling like I was crazy and broken.

Chapter 12

Trusting My Brilliance

It was days into October 2018, and I found my face glued to the window in the small single-row plane as it landed among the dramatic fall colors of the Rockies. I had made it to Montana. It didn't feel real. The potential for transformation that weekend wafted in the air like a meal being cooked far away, perceivable but not strong enough to decipher what was cooking. It intrigued me.

Since purchasing the airplane ticket less than two months earlier, my life had continued a metamorphosis. With the conclusion of the summer session, I'd packed up my office in the course of a few hours and loaded the boxes into my car. My long-time officemate and fellow bilingual speech-language pathologist was the only colleague to see me pack and leave. He and I had shared an office, a computer, woes, and joys for nine years. Over nearly a decade, we'd cultivated a unique empathetic understanding for one another. For the first five years of my tenure there, we were the only ones in our county with our jobs. No one else knew our jobs like we did. In those nine years, our busy schedules had kept us as ships passing each other in the port, but on that day, the last of the summer session, the universe orchestrated coordination. It was a tender and tearful send off.

Once home, I thoughtfully stored my boxes of books and therapy supplies in our garage. I wondered when I'd feel ready to provide, or ever be interested in providing direct speech-language services again.

I signed my new work contract in mid-September and was officially a clinical supervisor. I had a three-year temporary contract. Since signing, I'd attended a faculty meeting and been oriented to the school-age population I'd be supervising, graduate speech-language pathology students in their treating of clients. Sitting among former professors of mine as a peer-colleague, feelings of imposter syndrome ignited. Would I be smart enough to supervise cases and diagnoses that I had only seen or read about in graduate school a decade earlier? It would be new to be working with an older age group of clients. Instead of feeling less than for too long, I chose to be curious. I would embrace modeling the flexibility of our field to my students. With any career shift, there was a learning curve. My field was no different. I knew I would use my clinical experience to treat new issues and over time improve. Knowing that I had my upcoming trip to Montana before I signed my contract, I arranged my new work schedule around the trip.

Within the spacious white walled yoga studio in downtown Bozeman, Montana, a group of women began to celebrate being comfortable in our own skins. Surrounded by mothers of many forms, we all sought wholeness and connection as well as wellness and community. There was a three-hour gathering on the Friday night we all arrived. Waiting in the lobby of the yoga studio, bundled against the impending winter season, I eyed and smiled at people entering. Soon, eight, twelve, then over fifteen people were gathered in the space. Authors Molly Caro May, with her dark brown hair and silver earrings, and Kimberly Johnston, with her curly red hair and freckled face, came out to greet the group. Some women, in a surge of social-media-star-struck-awe fumbled to greet the two facilitators, as we filed into the studio space. The sun had set, and the dark night contrasted with the warm yellow glow of the studio lights. Participants got comfortable on yoga bolster pillows and blankets. We arranged ourselves in a huge circle. I took my seat to the right of Kimberly, who sat to the right of Molly. I was nervous and excited. Since high school, I'd kept various journals. Throughout my study-abroad program to Argentina, I acquired many lined spiraled notebooks from various liberías and corner botegas. The writing I had started in May, during my leave from work, and had resumed with regular dedication after the summer session, was different than journaling. This newer writing had been more therapeutic.

I'd never been to a workshop retreat like that before, and I didn't quite know what to expect. The joint-lead workshop was a first for Molly and Kimberly, as co-facilitators, too. I was open to doing deep work, like I had been in Ashland, and acknowledged that I arrived with various stages and ages of myself. We all made ourselves comfortable. In a fresh notebook of recycled paper, I made notes. "It's in the telling of the story that healing happens," Molly started, and I, and others, nodded in deep knowing. When I realized there was much to heal in my postpartum body, my postpartum story, I started writing. Hearing Molly state it outright affirmed my attraction to the event and settled any nagging nerves.

It was a joy listening to each person share their story: why they were here and what they hoped to get out of the weekend. We also completed three free-write prompts, my firsts ever. Molly gave us all a word, like "womanhood" or "sexuality," and then kept time for five or six minutes. In that space of time, we all scribed what came to mind and pen. There was magic—alchemy—in the writing.

Once time was called, I sat back and was a bit breathless and amused by what had come through me and out on the paper. It came from a place deep within myself. It was a truth-speaking place I wanted to keep visiting, a wellspring. Seeing my words that encompassed all of me—and feeling no shame in what went on the page—gave me a sense of peace and healing that I wanted more of. In those few moments of writing, I wove together a spectrum of feelings and thoughts that had surfaced, at various moments, in the last six-months. A glimpse of what I wrote:

Growing and stretching
Stretching to make marks on skin
Tire marks on roads with my peel outs
Enraged
Warm cuddly snuggles and stinky diapers
There were the real physical children and the one scared inside me
All three screaming and tugging for me until I'm swallowed whole.

Towards the end the first night, we all stood, shoulder to shoulder and read one after another one of our responses to the previous three prompts. Nervousness fluttered in my stomach and in my chest. As people read aloud it became clear everyone valued vulnerability and that steadied all our nerves. When the last women read, we stood in silence and then jazzy music turned on. We all stepped back, tucked notebooks and journals aside, and began to dance together before bidding goodnight. As I drove to my lodgings, a short drive away, I smiled and savored the sisterhood that was building among the group.

At nine o'clock the next day, we reunited and dove into the work. The hours passed quickly. Molly gave writing prompts about our five senses and used pages from children's picture books. These prompts had me processing moments of my past regarding my sister. We were then asked to crawl around the floor on all fours. I'd come to the workshop with an open mind to what unfolded in terms of activities. As I got down on my hands and knees, I was a little self-conscious but gave it my all. Kimberly informed us that crawling around was an entry point into experiencing our mammal bodies. The arch of the weekend workshop activities was well designed. We familiarized ourselves with our human nature and its relation to the making and sharing of stories. Then we reminded our bodies that we are animals. In doing so, we started learning how to listen to our bodies and the stories they told us to keep ourselves safe. The other women and I started to feel deeper into what it meant to have and move in a body. We touched one another's hands, shoulders, and backs. As a group, we growled, cried, yelled, and danced. It was as equally disorienting at times, as it was familiar and centring.

My body's felt sense of knowing revealed itself in the relaxing of tension in my shoulders and legs. That sensation quieted my mind's chatter about how bits of the workshop felt a bit awkward. Kimberly acquainted us with our nervous systems. She did that through a story, spoken and mimed, of a predator and its prey. In the center of our encircled hearts, she told us things our minds understood, like what it felt like to be stalked actually and energetically as women. She then showed us how we could—literally—shake off a sense of frozen fear, like prey animals do. In that instance, my eyes grew wide, and I finally understood why my body had, for as long as I could remember, twitched, like having a sort of tic, one or two times per day.

Kimberly went on to explain that spontaneous shivers, usually contractions of small muscle groups, were the nervous system calming itself and processing feelings. I was shocked, and I was equally thrilled. Since arriving, I felt I had so much to learn and was eager to do so. Sitting there now, I felt complete to finally understand something my body had done to support and help me. Shaking or shivering helps our bodies to digest life experiences, both the intense and mundane. It was mesmerizing hearing Kimberly speak, with lived experience behind her words. Listening to stories as a method of learning new information felt comforting to my mind and spirit.

With the sun setting in the west, I left the yoga studio to get dinner. Others were returning for an extra sensory-processing event with Kimberly, but I wanted to yield to what my body was shouting—REST! After getting some hot food from a natural food store, dark chocolate, and Epson salts, I drove to my Airbnb. I proceeded to unwind; I took a bath, watched a movie on my phone, and pondered all the writing prompts and somatic learning of the day. I lay there and started contemplating rest. It was emotionally painful yet freeing and necessary.

Why was it so hard to rest? The US is known for its fast paced everything. I could argue however that there was a micro, nano action in the slowing down, down regulation that was resting if that made me feel better. There was action in inaction. This insight gave me some permission from society to rest, some permission to stop and recharge. I fantasized that some hunter and gatherer communities, at one time, regarded rest for all, mothers especially, as a step in the dance of life. It was a part of organic sustainability. A plant doesn't continually flower or bear fruit. It's against nature. The same went for humans. Continual action, without rest, was a kind of prison sentence. Lack of rest caused physical damage to the body, mind, and soul.

It occurred to me that the ability to really rest was related to the amount of one's privilege. With more or less privilege, came degrees of allowed rest. But it should be enjoyed as a birthright. Indeed, Tricia Hersey, chaplain and founder of The Nap Ministry, declares that sleep deprivation is a social justice issue. I was aware of my privilege that night in Montana, and with privilege comes great responsibility. I rested for myself, and I rested for my ancestors.

As I wrote those thoughts down, I realized that my hesitation to slowing down, and the guilt I felt when I did put my feet up, came from my negative self-talk. I had internalized fast-paced capitalistic culture beliefs. Seeing both my parents work hard was additional evidence that productivity was important. My father's personal experience of being a migrant field worker and working in the rows of onions, strawberries, and potatoes by the age of five years old was both evidence of the importance of hard work and that he did not have time to adequately rest. My father's large family was the result of practical reasons, not religious ones. The larger the family, the more hands there were available to work the fields and earn money for the family. For the more marginalized, work also started early, and rest was not fathomable or affordable. I rested for him and field laborers like him.

My mother worked her way through college, earning $1-1.25 an hour, to complete two of the few degrees which were deemed appropriate for women at the time. By my age, she was divorced and a single parent with an adopted child from abroad, living in a new town with fifty dollars to her name. I rested for her and mothers like her.

My parents stayed busy even in retirement, even if they had slowed some. I would start to rest earlier in life rather than wait until retirement. Having reflected on my two lineages, I realized that they couldn't afford to rest as I could now. I melted into the flannel sheets of the oversized queen bed and drifted off to asleep.

The last morning of the retreat swirled with lament that the workshop was ending and curiosity of what might be revealed before departing. For the final exercise of somatic work, we paired off around the circle. I was paired with a woman from San Diego. She had short grey hair and had worked with Kimberly before. In the activity, each pair was asked to interlock hands, push against each other, and vocalize all at once. We were guided to find our animal voice and let it out. Naturally, pushing up against resistance, a guttural growl emerged out of my throat. With more pressure applied to my partner's hands, the volume increased. My partner in turn was finding her voice and letting it sound.

While pairs around the room erupted in various harmonies and intensities, Kimberly walked among us. She approached our pairing. I had been feeling proud of my tone and the volume of my animal voice. I was proud of my body. Next, Kimberly placed both her hands gently on both my hips and held them there for a few seconds. In that short span of time, it was as if a spark of energy, a spark of my true self, ping-ponged down from my throat, where it had been sounding loud and strong, down between my hips, tinkled down my knees, and landed in the soles of my feet, all the while rendering me mute. Kimberly moved to another pairing, and I locked eyes with my partner. I gripped her hands now to steady myself, and I slowly crumpled to the floor. When the energy had reached my feet, it left an illuminated trail throughout my body, as if telling my mind that "all this, too, is yours to inhabit, all of this." My first vocalizations had only been coming from half of me, from my diaphragm up to my head. With Kimberly's touch, my body remembered all the rest of itself, down to my soles. That was how much space my soul really took up in my body.

Slumped on the light-colored bamboo floor, I started to sob. It was a mix of relief, grief, and a myriad of feelings I could not consciously name in the moment. My partner comforted me by patting my rounded back. After a minute or so, I stood up again, with her help. I honored my emotions and wanted to find my voice again. My partner and I began anew with our hands interlocked and pressing into one another. My voice now cracked, squeaked, and birthed itself awkwardly until a steady, low tone was achieved. The newfound cry traveled up from my feet, through my torso and diaphragm, and out between my vocal cords and my lips. My new animal voice resonated throughout my entire body.

The power of touch has always astonished me. Sometimes the brain needs a different kind of input to make sense of what goes on within it. After the retreat closed, I drove my rental car back to the airport to catch my early afternoon flight, and as I did, I could feel my frozen self begin its overdue thaw. Sitting in a window seat again, I recalled swaying among the other women on the journey into our forgotten bodies. The process of change that took place among the group resembled a sort of cleansing ceremony. Each participant collected, uplifted, and offered beliefs, habits, thoughts, and actions into the greater circle. Faces, postures, and limbs looked different after our time together. While I admired views of the Rocky Mountains, the scale of our collective release burned and shined in my mind. The processes had refined us all to a golden brilliance. Molly said on Friday to "trust your own brilliance." She was so right, and I felt brave enough to start trusting.

Back home, something felt changed within me. It was like I'd taken a muscle relaxer. My whole body felt loose and flexible. My arms hung freely, my shoulders were down, and my digestion was great—it was a kind of miracle. I didn't want it to end. A week later, walking down the hall at work, and I still felt similarly de-stressed. My mind-body learned what it meant and what it felt like to have my nervous system become calmer. It was heavenly. The internal storm of feeling overwhelmed could be soothed and regulated. Could I keep it up?

Since learning the specific cues of the nervous systems from Kimberly, I recognized in my body when a stress storm was beginning to brew. As the fall season changed into winter, I began to listen more to my body and utilized what I had invested in myself in Montana. I would continue to follow the guideposts of my body's cues to help inform my thinking mind. Over time, it saved my household from enduring more destructions and my heart from feeling more guilt and shame. With practice, I noticed when I was crabby and needed to eat. In those moments, I told my little girls: "Mommy needs to take care of herself first. Please be patient. I love you, and Mommy loves Mommy." On days when I knew I would be caregiving without Luke, I would think of things to do with the girls that brought me joy and were in sync with my physical energy that day. If I were nearing my menstrual period, and also caregiving alone, I planned movie time for us or a playdate for Corazón so I would be sure to do less and rest at a time in the month when I knew I had the least resources. Instead of pushing to think of and make dinner after work on busy days, I coordinated with Luke, and we ordered delivery. I was proud to be positioning myself centrally in my mothering.

As 2018 wound to a close, I noticed grey hairs sprouting from my head. It had been eight months since the acute collapse of my health, supermom life as I'd known it, and my leave of absence. It would be a slow recovery. It would be a work in progress. Hearing illegal fireworks blast in our neighborhood, I sat up and watched the bedside clock turn over from 11:59 p.m. on January 31, 2018, to 12:00 a.m. January 1, 2019. And then I sighed an audible sound of relief. 2018 had been an arduous year for me, and I was thankful to end it with new hope and new tools.

The waves of fatigue, anxiety, and depression that continued in smaller stints in the early months of 2019 reminded me that I'd given life twice. I'd used—gifted—my life force and I will never have some of it again. I would learn to hold the magnitude of my sacrifice with tenderness and that was what I did when I practiced resting. It took me having two children and thirty-five years to understand, with all the cells in my body, the energy it takes for the rosebush to produce a single flower.

Chapter 13

Postpartum/365

All the various writing prompts the group completed at the workshop in Montana showed me glimpses into myself and into my writing capabilities that made me want to do it more. After the workshop had ended, and people lingered to talk and have books signed by Kimberly and Molly, I got a chance to talk with Molly. Standing among chatting dyads and small groups, I asked Molly to sign her book for me. I told her that after purchasing her book, I'd started writing my mental health experiences down. I'd done it like therapy and had a few pieces I didn't quite know what to do with and wondered if she did any coaching. She said she did and to email her once I got home. I was a new level of happy and asked a new acquaintance to take our picture before I left to catch my flight home. After checking into my flight and waiting at the gate with large vistas of the mountains leading to Yellowstone National Park, I looked at the picture of Molly and me. I almost didn't recognize myself. I looked different, which confirmed to me the seismic shifts I felt inside.

When I got home after dark from my Montana trip, the girls were in bed, and Luke was eager to hear about my weekend. After I shared the visceral experiences, he asked, "What's next for you, honey?" His supportive question filled my already excited self with soft energy. I wanted more opportunities to "trust my own brilliance," as Molly had said, so I talked with Luke about what he thought of me working with Molly as a writing coach and mentor. Luke had seen me pore over my laptop keys after a particularly challenging afternoon and come away with more clarity and calm. He had supportively listened to some of what I wrote. Luke loved the idea. Leaning into my self-trust with what felt like blind faith, I authored a follow-up email to Molly. In it, I asked if she would read a piece and give me some feedback. She agreed, and I sent her some of my writing not even two weeks after the workshop. What followed was the beginning of a mentoring relationship and the groundwork for this book.

The new year of 2019 opened before me like a blank canvas. The tools I'd been collecting since May, plus the new material I was oriented to in Montana in October, became new habits. Body scanning to gauge what I needed so I could return to a centred sense of myself was something I did almost hourly. When Corazón asserted herself, and I wanted to return similar four-year-old sass, I recognized my inner child had showed up, and I stepped in to navigate.

With my clinical supervising job, I didn't work full time, which allowed me to continue treating the adrenal fatigue by taking various supplements and actively managing my mental health with regular counseling and acupuncture. Writing regularly continued to be part of my healing journey. I met with Molly monthly on the phone to review the pieces I'd submitted to her. My writing was improving, and my investment in myself was novel. It felt so gratifying to be building a skillset. For two hours, most Fridays for six months, I wrote in the vaulted-ceilinged, granary-turned-coffee-shop across the street from the city jail and kiddy corner to my reiki minister friend's studio. I relished the spring of words that flowed from within me, as I entered a sanctum of myself. It was precious time spent with myself before I'd have to move on and pick up Corazón from kindergarten. If ideas came to me mid-week, I entered them on an app in my phone. A creative tempo developed alongside my own honoring of my menstrual rhythm. Resting was also part of the cycle. On some Fridays, I lay on our grey couch and napped or meditated for a second time. Writing, resting, and retuning myself to my needs became the interior design of my life.

As spring approached, and the one-year anniversary of my pulling the emergency brake on life with my leave from work, Molly happened to announce a new online workshop: Heal Your Postpartum Story. Like muscle memory, my body tensed as the later days in April approached. As if an alarm of sorts was set within me, I was acutely aware of the date, how I was feeling, and tried to measure my progress of the changes in our family and myself over the last year, all 365 days of it. Reading the writing workshop description was like a massage. In celebration of having made it a whole year since the "Great Rearranging," I signed up. I was hopeful that just as much mending of myself would happen in that course as happened in Montana.

For five weeks, I joined mothers from across the US and Europe online. We attended group-writing sessions and had access to an online chat forum. There was so much healing in hearing other stories. Molly guided the group through themes each week. One of them was proportionality. She challenged us to consider what we had forgotten or left out when we thought of, retold, or gave an account of our postpartum story. There were many reasons why events, kind actions, or good things were not included in our stories. She explained that our stories served a purpose for us and depending on how we framed them, unconsciously, that would help or hurt our cause. At the start of the prompt, "What did you forget?" I waited, pen poised above the same journal I had used in Montana six months earlier. Feeling the containment of the six-minute time limit, I scanned my postpartum memory with Juliet like someone scanning a pitch-black room for their bearings. And then, like lightning, memories flashed in my mind, loud and fast.

On an early-November morning in 2016, I woke to waves of debilitating nausea. I was six weeks pregnant. The green queasy grip on my stomach, which summoned the urge to retch up my throat, was similar to week six of Corazón's pregnancy. Relying on past experience, I got bland crackers to have at my bedside to eat before lifting my head from the pillow. I bought mouthwash because brushing my teeth would be intolerable, and I wondered how I would parent a two-year-old while feeling so horrid.

With each subsequent week, there was no relief in sight, and my tolerance for the nausea was waning. By that point, I'd started the remedy from my mother's cousin, a highly experienced midwife, of vitamin B6 and an over-the-counter sleeping pill. I had hopes that that would soothe the rough seas that churned in my belly and swelled to take me all the way to bed. Yet there was a hint of pleasure in my suffering. Wasn't it all a good sign? The nausea felt different, stronger. Thanksgiving came that year, and I only survived because I lay in the window seat in my in-laws' living room, feeling miserable. As the weeks went on like that, I wondered if some counseling wouldn't be wise, too.

At that time, there was a skilled clinical social worker available to me at my office of special education providers. The short, small-framed woman was a real healer. I'd utilized her services before as part of the grant-funded project our agency participated in. Our times together were always surprisingly magical. In the small conference room, upstairs, with two large windows, time expanded, and insights flooded in like breaths of fresh air. Clarity was her sidekick. That wasn't just my experience but that of my colleagues as well. In our conversation on a crisp day in early December, a novel truth came knocking: I had not processed my miscarriage, my first pregnancy, prior to getting pregnant with Corazón. That insight left me gasping and dumbfounded. Deep into my core, I now understood the grip that was around my uterus. It had felt linked to my nausea. I met grief, some two years after the fact, and it made me double over.

The social worker suggested I learn the emotional freedom technique to help my nervous system and my body come into present time versus remaining stuck and fearful of losing another baby—the one I now carried. My fear had made me sicker, to the point of needing prescription antinausea medication. What the social worker said made sense, and I felt lighter and hopeful. At home that evening, I searched online for the tapping technique that the social worker had suggested could help my nausea and began a daily practice. I tapped on each side of my collarbone, between my eyes, and so on. Over the course of a few days, my nausea reduced by two thirds. I couldn't believe it. The tapping allowed me to scale back on the medication some days; by week's end, I had stopped taking it completely. While tapping, I felt truths resurrect themselves, as if the steady touch of my fingertips wrote a message of remembering in body morse code. I'd lost my first pregnancy. I was heartbroken. Getting pregnant a third time was anxiety provoking but had worked out. I was scared. I told myself: "I can have a healthy pregnancy and not feel as though I need to throw up all my insides. Imposed suffering is not going to save you from miscarrying again."

As Molly called time on the six-minute write, I was teleported back to the online workshop and felt a little dizzy. I was shocked that I had forgotten how sick I'd been with Juliet's pregnancy and the lingering grief of my miscarriage. Some participants took turns and shared forgotten bits of their stories before we continued with another writing session. The prompt was a breeze of fresh air in a stale room of myself. With the final prompt of that week, there was a whole other wing of my inner home that had its curtains unfastened and windows flung open: my sister and her fertility journey.

When I was twenty-six, my sister married for a second time at thirty-five. She made great efforts to connect with me and bridge the age gap, as well as the time zones, over the years. We even created our own holiday, "Sister's Day," in the summer months and exchanged gifts to celebrate, often by mail. With our age difference and occupying different life stages, the timing of our marrying six months apart gave me hope of more closeness. Little did we both know that when I was thirty-five, our lives would be diametrically opposed.

The same week in November of 2013 that Luke and I learned our baby was a girl, my sister and her husband learned he was sterile. My sister and her husband made another pregnancy plan involving a sperm donor and IVF, which started with timely shots and detailed protocols. Meanwhile, Luke and I navigated changing diapers and adjusted to parenthood with Corazón. A year later, on her fortieth birthday, she was pregnant for a short time before miscarrying. My soul was crushed. All that work, all that money, and all that waiting left my sister with an empty womb and extra weight from the hormone shots. Soon, her marriage suffered, and by the time Juliet was born, she was three months divorced.

I had hoped when we each got married six months apart, and she and her husband planned to also live on the West Coast, we would have more in common. Would I finally have a warm and fuzzy sisterly relationship that would heal years of all kinds of distances? Instead, we lived lives neither of us expected. And IVF wasn't the end of it.

Juliet was seven months old, and I was at work when she called with her news: My sister had cervical cancer. Time stopped, and my heart broke for her, again. Juliet was eight months old, wearing her pink cast, when my sister had a hysterectomy. Her reproductive fate was sealed forever. She would never be a biological mother, and we would never be sisters and mothers together. It was as though my sister and I lived on two different planets in the same galaxy of our family.

Looking down at my writing, I watched a wet circle spread in the margin. My eyes were wet with sadness and frustration. For all the support I craved and needed during those days and months that I struggled with hot feelings of irritation, depression, and rage as a parent, I didn't call her for comfort. I feared she would hear my venting about the challenging reality of motherhood as complaining. From the outside, I had everything: a husband and kids. My sister would have been happy for me, I'm sure, but I didn't want to offend her or hurt her more than life had already. In my trying to get through the stormy unexpected postpartum depression and anxiety, I had not the fortitude to also incorporate her storyline into my own. It was so sad, and I was helpless to support her.

The five-week online class passed quickly. There were video adlibs where participants opened up about their vulnerable mothering experiences. In the community forum, there was the giving and receiving of free-writing feedback. Through our unpacking of one another's stories throughout the course, I felt a sense of community—one that I'd longed for. I found other women who wanted to explore their postpartum stories with curiosity and the possibility of healing. Many became my heart-sister friends. Molly's rhythm of prompts and sharing was restorative. She said: "Humans are story makers and hearers. Story making and telling regulates our nervous systems." At the conclusion of the workshop, she encouraged us to take these free-write prompts, or others we made up, out to our communities. That gave me an idea. I wanted to try hosting mother-writing circles of my own.

Flexing some creative muscles, I designed an attractive flier for a two-hour writing gathering a few weeks later, at the end of June. I was nervous as the sun set slowly on the Thursday evening of the meeting. Women arrived, in staggered pairs, until there were six of us total. We sat on blankets, writing supplies to our sides, in a circle on the bamboo floors of the group acupuncture space at Luke's office. Therapy tables were shoved off to the sides to open a space for us to gather.

To start, I shared about finding Molly's book a year earlier and my most recent workshop with her. I explained I was not a counselor nor would I give any coaching; the space was intended to support writing and exploring what we wrote. If someone wanted to read what they wrote aloud, they were invited, and it was clarified that no writing critiques or suggestions would be made. What people could share as feedback was how a phrase or word stood out to them or what the listener was curious to learn more about. By the end of the gathering, all in attendance agreed that some healing alchemy happened for them and that making and sharing stories were surprisingly comforting to them too. Regular free-write meetings like this one became another source of support and community for me.

2019 brought opportunities to continue to heal and fortify myself. When Luke also worked on weekends, we planned ahead with baby-sitters, our nanny, or made arrangements with my parents to support me with the caregiving. Asking for support didn't shame me or cause me guilt as it had before. I reminded myself that good mothers ask for help and that guilt's sticky grip would loosen and fade.

I honored my needs daily, as I could, and was happier as a mother when I put my needs beside those of my children. To help myself make the shift, and keep up caring about myself, I stated aloud to my girls, while moving around the kitchen some mornings, that "Mommy's getting crabby and needs to eat," as I'd grab the eggs for my own breakfast before theirs. Over time, it became my first inclination to nourish myself and not feel it was selfish. I used television time for the girls when I needed some quiet or to take a rest and then enjoyed drawing, dressing up, and cooking with my daughters when I had more energy. Some days were a challenge, as my inner negative voice would blast, and I would feel discouraged. I was regularly rewiring myself and taking a broader view of the situations of my postpartum mental health as well as my ongoing mental health. I now saw how each year, each three-hundred-sixty-five days I completed another cycle of my post-partum time. So much had changed for the better in one year.

The mother-writer friends I gained from Molly's courses, like me, also worked on themselves to regulate their nervous systems. They worked to exhale long when their children annoyed them by asking for three things at once or when they experienced skin-scrawling agitation from the mundane tasks of caregiving nine hours a day. As summer waned, I was eager to transition into autumn by writing in a group again, in person if possible. Upon learning Molly planned to hold a weekend workshop in November, I made plans to travel again to Montana and booked the same Airbnb room for continuity and security.

Snowy streets welcomed me upon my arrival to Bozeman. Returning for a second year in a row was comforting. Maybe that's what migrating birds felt like when they roosted in familiar spots on annual migrations? This had become mine, and it made me happy. For two-and-a-half days, the upper rooms inside a church provided another type of sanctuary for me and seven other women. One other woman came from out of state. Her husband had found Molly's book and workshops, and the couple had driven from Washington so she could have a community experience. The theme for the workshop was our postpartum stories, and a lovely sign made from the hand-carved print image of a winged uterus and ovaries, created by one of the participants, greeted me at the back door of the church.

We worked at a long, wooden table, pulling our chairs around it. The windows faced north and filtered in cool light through snow-covered branches. Various crystal sun catchers hung among the panes. That wall of light, changing with the time of day, became another member of the group as we wrote that weekend. With the small group size, there was ample time to share our stories. Over the course of the weekend, we paired up in different combinations, read around the table, or read at random when someone felt called to share. Some mothers were taking the time of the weekend workshop, as a first time, to make and take up space for themselves. These women had babies six or eight months old and their hearts and breasts experienced visceral expansions and contractions. Again, medicine was cultivated through each of our writing prompts for each woman and as a group. We navigated through various emotional terrains alongside one another. Many of us were new to free writing, and once more, Molly assured us to "trust your own brilliance."

I had learned so much since being in Montana the year before. Although the prompts were very similar to the online, five-week course I'd taken in the spring, writing among people was otherworldly. The walls of that room generated a needed womblike space for us mothers to recollect and reflect on the lives we created as well as the people we were becoming. It was a sacred time and space. I felt steady within myself and appreciated the ability to contrast those feelings with what I felt the year before. I had created a ritual of writing, my own personal season, and I planned to make space for it annually.

Starting back in the summer, I kept my head, and shoulders at times, above the waters of motherhood with new ability. Luke and I were optimistic about my improved physical and mental health and made plans for an end of the year trip to Southern California. It would be our first trip with just the four of us. He and I planned it together to ensure its success.

In the dark of early morning, on the day after Christmas, we woke the girls and loaded them into the car, still in their pajamas; Corazón was five, and Juliet was almost two and a half. Our early flight would grant us more time in sunny LA, or so we planned. Waiting in the restaurant that was adjacent to the boarding area for our gate, Luke and I colored on the kids' placemats and took enjoyment in the present moment. An announcement on the intercom said our flight was delayed due to icy conditions at the plane's point of origin. Undiscouraged, we moved the family to an empty corner of the boarding area and made up games of hopping, dancing, and skipping to pass the time. With the sky brightening in the west, from the sun pouring over the eastern hills as it rose, we learned our flight was now so delayed that we would miss our connection to LA. The airline rebooked us on an afternoon flight; scheduled for 4:20 p.m. Luke was beyond frustrated. We'd been looking forward to this vacation for months. I was so disappointed we'd gotten the kids up so early for nothing. Luke was going to get us there faster, he said. He got out his phone and dialed the airline.

Leaving the airport parking lot, he was on hold with the airline, still. Driving us down the highway toward home, to wait for our flight there, I suggested Luke call on my phone, too, to see who got through faster. After two minutes, someone came on the line. Since my phone got an answer, Luke hung up, and I pulled over. Within minutes, we were headed back to the airport and were scheduled to leave on a different flight, with hopes of making the connection and arriving that afternoon in LA by 5:00 p.m.

The yo-yo feeling of the morning left my head whirling, but my mood calm as the new flight took off. I settled into my worn leather seat and took some deep breaths. We would first fly north to Seattle and then south to LA. The time passed easily; the novelty of the flight kept the girls entertained, along with a few of their new gifts. With a bump, the wheels touched down, and Luke and I were flooded with a sense of urgency. Our next flight was due to board, and we still needed to get to the gate. We worried we'd be stuck in Seattle. Quickly, we decided that he and Corazón would get up as soon as the seatbelt sign went off and run to our next gate in hopes to hold the flight. Our flight attendants knew that our connection would be tight and supported our efforts to exit quickly. Juliet and I would hurry along behind. As Luke and Corazón rushed down the narrow aisle, I hoisted Juliet up onto my back and strapped the soft brown carrier around myself. We shimmied between people getting up from their seats, and then we were out and walking up ramps to the concourse. I tried jogging, but the weight of Juliet had me winded in a few steps. "We need to catch up with daddy and sister!" I said just as much to her as to myself.

The shiny grey metal beams and glass concourse looked all the same to my right and to my left. My chest tightened a little, and I felt sweat beading up on my forehead. I focused on keeping my breath even while I quickly checked the departures board and the current gate to ensure I was headed in the right direction. Again, I tried fast walking, even jogging, to make time, but after a few gates, I knew I wouldn't make it, as I was already sweating. I started looking around and listening for one of the little carts that carried disabled passengers to their gates. I was desperate. I spotted one just a few feet behind me. Breathless, I waved the driver to stop and asked for a ride. The older driver, seeing Juliet peering over my shoulder said, "Sure, get in!" Even though the cart was slow moving, it moved much faster than I would have been able to move with a twenty-pound child on my person. Sweat had dampened my back and underarms from carrying Juliet and running. I worked on catching my breath and was hoping beyond hope we'd make our flight as a family.

Our gate appeared on the right. Luke and Corazón were there, catching their breath, at the ticket counter adjacent to the main door, with the boarding attendant. The flight hadn't left. There was hope of finally arriving to sunny California before the day's end. I lumbered up to them. Juliet was still on my back when she announced, "Tengo caca!" Crestfallen, I stopped in my tracks and thought *A potty stop? Now!? We don't have time, and she can't wait.* My body started to get hot, and panic itched down my face. So much had happened in the eight hours since I woke up, and Juliet's need for a toilet almost rendered me immobile. Overhearing my plight, a mother waiting in the area for the next flight called out, "I have a diaper. What size do you need?" Juliet had been potty trained for some months, and I didn't pack diapers, instead relishing the extra space for toys. "Any size you have will be great," I said. "Thank you!" I wove between short banks of seats and got the diaper from her. "Good luck!" she offered as I took it from her and quickly turned to board the plane. Down the jetway, through the main door, and into our seats, I had Juliet squat down and quickly use the clean diaper to go potty before buckling her in. I mentally applauded myself for packing wipes, which were intended for faces and noses. Our seats were in the back row. Luke and I were on either side of the girls like bookends. We chuckled at each other and shook our heads in disbelief. We'd made it! As the plane pushed back, I marveled: "What a day, and it's only lunchtime!"

The rollercoaster ride of traveling to our long-awaited vacation finally delivered us safe and sound—four hours later than our original reservation. But flexibility was the name of the parenting game. Upon arriving, we quickly enjoyed our clever planning—a camper van served as our rental car. The snacks I'd packed lasted. The screen and nonscreen travel activities had succeeded for entertainment. Familiar road signs and barren bluffs of the Santa Monica Mountains calmed me as we found our lodgings just after sunset.

Luke and I balanced individual alone time with family time, and the week was surprisingly enjoyable. The camper van provided easy cooking options at the beach where we played, and Luke surfed. We rented a kid-sized wetsuit for Corazón, and she got some surf lessons with her dad. The van's seat beds allowed for quiet, shaded nap times for all, and the pop-up table provided coloring and Lego playing space when the sun was too strong. Our family made memories: we made banana pancakes with an ocean view, ran down the beach in the morning, played with magnet shapes in the half-dome beach tent on the sand, and played hide-and-seek in the high-ceilinged Airbnb with purple quartz counters. Luke and I decided to go back to the same beach each day because why change something that worked? Taking time to notice and savor those magical moments we had together helped to salve the previous year's turbulent times.

Among colorful swings, slides, and padded-surface play spaces, my family and I gathered to watch the last sunset of 2019. The sky was cloudless and started to glow with pinks and blues. Near the Venice Boardwalk, other families also watched the symbolic passage of time. That whole year was one where I breathed more deeply and listened more attentively to my body and its needs. A warm gentle pride filled my chest as I linked arms with Luke, and we jointly pushed our girls on the swings. Continuing to yield to myself was my resolution. 2020 would be a new opportunity to keep growing into myself as a person and as a mother. The new year didn't frighten, discourage, or overwhelm me—it was a much welcomed change. We'd lived in and through the eye of a severe storm, and it had passed. With time, more healing would happen, and I would come to expect the unexpected.

Acknowledgments

Writing this book originally was another therapeutic process to assimilate the unexpected postpartum challenges I faced throughout 2018. Like me, this project has shifted and changed and ultimately grew into a work all its own. I'd like to thank my early draft(s) readers Jackie, Sarah O. and Sarah B., Emily, Dr. De Anda, Megan, and others, whose thoughtful questions challenged me and transformed this project. To my peer supporters Cath, Gursharn, Rebecca, Saadia, and Suzy—my writing-mama sisters: thank you for being my sounding boards and readers as well as for offering me encouragement during the editing process. Your hugs and/or text messages sent in sparse moments of free time, were infusions of motivation that traveled across many time zones. Your collective valuing of the healing power of giving voice to one's stories has been nourishing. Melissa McCoubrey, your editing support of the final manuscript validated my story. And a big thank you to my Demeter Press copy editor Jesse O'Reilly-Conlin, now my book sparkles.

Molly Caro May, your work, in book form, in person, or online, has helped me heal. Thank you for your coaching, endless cheering on, and for your motto "trust your own brilliance." It often brings me back to my midline, my centered self. I savor our parallel journeys into the nervous systems, through various means, and regular writing touchpoints. Your example of holding creativity and wellness in a state of synchrony with the undulation of life is a comfort to me and to many others.

To my various care providers—Dr. Iglesias Wheeler, Dr. Edwards, Dr. Reilly, and Dr. Yates—your collective wisdom and care shaped my journey to wellness. Dr. Serrallach's book *The Postnatal Depletion Cure* has also been a source of guidance.

Luke, your friendship, unconditional love, and unwavering support are foundational to me. Your faith in me and this project have been essential ingredients—thank you. To my parents, Rafael and Cathy, who have been steady companions on my life's journey, thank you for supporting our family with childcare, especially during 2020–2021 and the pandemic so I could have space to write and rest. Thank you to my sister, Kia, for your unwavering belief in my achievements, including this book.

During a ten-week motherhood studies course with motherhood scholar and sociologist Dr. Sophie Brock in the spring of 2021, I had the pleasure of meeting pioneer scholar of Motherhood Studies, and Demeter Press originator, Dr. Andrea O'Reilly on a Q&A call. From her living room couch over zoom, she said candidly, "I created it [matricentric feminism] out of necessity," and I knew just what she meant. Hearing her answer our questions about why she formulated the concept of matricentric feminism convinced me that her press was a good home for my story. I wrote my story, this book, out of necessity. I'm so thankful and am honored to have Demeter Press as my publisher.

During the editing process of the final manuscript, I completed a two-day course with Postpartum Support International (PSI) titled Perinatal Mood Disorders: Components of Care. Within the first hour of the course, tears ran down my cheeks. Learning diagnostic criteria for perinatal depression and anxiety disorders brought memories of seasonal depression and anxiety as well as postpartum agitation, rage, sadness, and depression flooding back to me. By lunchtime, I was awestruck to learn, and really piece together, that I had, since my teens, experienced many of what the course listed as contributing health factors that increased a woman's risk of experiencing a perinatal mood and anxiety disorder (PMAD) beyond their race. These memories gave me more ideas for chapters to write with hopes of showing a longer-range trajectory of my health issues. The PSI education also gave me much knowledge, which I've shared at state and national level professional conferences for speech-language pathologists working with young families and children in hopes of helping more families.

Although it was unknown to me during my time of great struggle, PSI is an amazing organization and is dedicated to supporting and educating families and society on PMADs. Get support and learn more at www. postpartum.net

And thank you to my daughters, who at publication are eight and five. The months and weeks that my story, our story, took place are forever etched into our hearts and psyches. I see that with time, and new skills we've been healing together. Thank you for growing along with me in the innate messiness that is learning, living, and loving. You two are my greatest teachers and it's my heart's delight to be your mother, teacher, and friend.